ROBERT R. SCHUTZ, Ph.D.

THE
$30,000
SOLUTION

Fithian Press
SANTA BARBARA • 1996

To my mother,
who always wanted me to help
make the world a better place.

Copyright ©1996 by Robert R. Schutz, Ph.D.
All rights reserved.
Printed in the United States of America.

Design and typography by Jim Cook

Published by Fithian Press,
a division of Daniel & Daniel, Publishers, Inc.,
Post Office Box 1525, Santa Barbara, California 93102

LIBRARY OF CONGRESS CATALOGING-IN-PUBLICATION DATA
Schutz, Robert R.
The $30,000 solution / Robert R. Schutz.
p.   cm.
Includes bibliographical references and index.
ISBN 1-56474-150-8 (pbk. : alk. paper)
1. Distribution (Economic theory)
2. Guaranteed annual income—United States.
3. Population policy.   I. Title.
HB523.S38   1996
362.5'82—dc20   95-31327
CIP

THE $30,000 SOLUTION

Contents

Preface

This book is the result of forty years' observation of and reflection on the economic system. The system is a great production machine, but it has problems in the way it distributes income and treats the earth, our home.

This is a fix-it book, and a how-to book. It asks you to change your mind on "the way things always have been." It is a book about freedom, fairness, and democracy. It will make you wealthy as it eliminates poverty and welfare. And it will stabilize the dollar.

It will enable us to live lightly on the earth. And it will provide good work.

The system is unfair

This book proposes that the system is unfair, both to the poor and the rich. And it proposes a solution that would be fairer. It divides the income we receive into two familiar categories: earned and unearned.

We work for the former, and we don't work for the latter.

There are lots of both kinds of income in the system.

Unearned income belongs to us all

The suggestion here offered is that no one has any more right to unearned income than anyone else.

In order to make our system of income distribution fair, we have to equalize the income that is derived from not working, while we allow workers to be paid according to their ability, skill, training, and output.

The same program will work for the environment

Fortunately, the very means we use to make ourselves well off will make it possible for us to save the world from human destruction. We have a few short years in which to live up to our fine name. (*Homo sapiens* means "wise person.") Less than a century in which to turn around the whole system, and make ourselves benign as well as fair.

We have priorities

Since we have all been trained to greed, we will start first with making ourselves better off, and, second, take up our desire to leave a world for our children. "Greed" is a bad word. We don't like to think this of ourselves. But it is true of most of us, a part of our conditioning. Perhaps looking out for ourselves is more palatable. Or security. Or prudence. Whatever we call it, a little bit may be a good thing. Only when it becomes an addiction is it harmful, both to ourselves and to others. Then it needs to be limited.

Leaving a bountiful world to our children is not second in importance. There will be no riches if we have few resources.

I simply see no way to save the world by direct attacks on big greed with a thousand points of light. Perhaps we can harness little greed in the service of the world. Perhaps we can find there, in ourselves, the key to a way forward.

One remedy for two big problems

In this book, we will find that the same process works for both problems.

Preface

If we work for fair income for everyone, we will at the same time save the environment.

Simple, straightforward, and right

This seems like a simple, straightforward, ultimately right and fair solution to an awkward problem. If we follow it out, a number of fine corollaries will appear, such as:

1. No more poverty
2. No more homelessness
3. Far less crime
4. No unemployment or inflation
5. Little or no discrimination on the basis of race or sex
6. Less environmental degradation
7. And a happy work force

You will see how it works! I hope you enjoy the book, too.

ACKNOWLEDGEMENTS

I have had lots of help in preparing this manuscript. No one makes a leap or even an inch of forward progress in thinking without standing on the shoulders of hundreds of other thinkers and doers in the world.

I would like particularly to thank Bernie Kirby, UCSD sociologist, who bounced ideas back and forth with me and read every word of many versions before he died of cancer in 1992; Trevor Thomas, a skillful editor who imposed a better turn of phrase with every reading of the many drafts he has been over; economists Kenneth Boulding and Jack Powelson, whose sometimes scorching comments have enlightened me and made the product better.

Herman Daly and Hazel Henderson and Ted Roszak and Bob Heilman and Ted Roth, teachers who have encouraged me to continue when publication seemed remote; Betty Bacon, Charlie Varon, Fran Peavey, Paul Johnson and dozens of others including classes I've taught at Sacramento State University, Santa Rosa Junior College, and Friends General Conference Gatherings.

All have been immensely helpful; but, of course, I am the one who takes responsibility for any errors of fact and interpretation. I expect you, the reader, to approach this thesis with all of your critical intelligence, and hope you will come to conclusions similar to mine at the end of the book.

Chapter 1.
A few questions that may
occur to the reader

If I, the author, answer some of the questions you may have at the outset, you will be able to "see where I'm coming from."

Thus, we may both be able to check our assumptions, to see if they fit, and to see if we can proceed from here to mutually agreeable conclusions.

First, what is the total amount we are talking about?

Unearned income adds up to $30,000, every year, for every U.S. citizen.

Isn't that an awful lot of money?

It certainly is. It is more than anyone needs for a frugal lifestyle. But it is there, and we have to decide what to do with it. This is four times the poverty level. It is not subsistence, which other writers on a "basic income" strive for.

Wealthy people don't think $30,000 is much money. We may have to begin to think like wealthy people.

How do you know that it's "there"?

Here is an approximation that checks it. If we divide the gross national product by the population, $6 trillion divided by 250 million people is $24,000 per year. This is in the ball park.

Of course the gross national product is not the national income. And neither does it count a lot of things, like the "underground" economy, or rent on owner-occupied property. And we don't propose to give children the same amount we allow for adults.

But GNP is in the ball park. And when we figure it all out, unearned income comes to a little more than $30,000, per adult citizen, per year.

Isn't it wrong to give poor people $30,000 per year for just living and being citizens?

We have been conditioned to think so. They say John Smith told the pilgrims, "If you don't work, you don't eat." That fit well with his Puritan background. If the Pilgrims had not landed on Plymouth rock, but instead in the Garden of Eden, with breadfruit and bananas and pineapples lying all about, he might have said something else.

How about, "We will divide up what is given, and if you want more, you have to work for it?"

Where are we now, on the rocks or in the Garden of Eden? We presently give the money that is unearned to a few people, who are then "rich," or wealthy. Is this "right?" This book doesn't propose giving it to the poor, by the way, but to everyone.

How did you arrive at the "magic figure," $30,000 per year?

All of the unearned income, carefully estimated, divided by the number of people, adjusted by a lower amount for children, gives more than $30,000 per adult per year in 1990. Earned income also comes in for scrutiny, with a cap on very high salaries.

How do you define earned and unearned income? Do I earn an income for managing my own investments, for example?

Earned is payment for work. Unearned is payment for no

work. Unearned income includes interest, rent, capital gains, dividends, gambling and lottery winnings, the rewards of crime and embezzlement, gifts, inheritance—every bit of money you get without having to lift a finger for it.

Crime could be described as work, but we will stick with legitimate payment. If managing your own investments yields enough income to pay you a salary, by all means take it, up to, say, 10 percent of the yield. The same for "managing" (i.e., collecting the rent and seeing to maintenance and paying the bills) on your own property.

This management option is one reason we put a cap on salary. You can get rich on salary, but don't count on it to substitute for the income from a billion dollars worth of stocks and bonds.

You listed rent as an example of unearned income. Does this mean that your project is a warmed-over version of Henry George, whose ideas were thrown out a century ago?

Henry George lived more than a century ago, but many of his ideas are still flourishing today, even among a few economists.

George recognized land as the ultimate monopoly, since there is just so much, and no more can be created by humans. He would have us tax land to the limit of its income, rent, and thought this would yield enough to run the government, leaving the rest of our economy untaxed.

This project extends George by recognizing many other types of monopoly, many artificial shortages created by humans that ought to be similarly taxed. They result in unearned income, even more than we need to run a government bloated by arms expenditures and entitlements.

This income must be divided equally among us in order to be fair to all of us.

What is "fair" about soaking the rich on their hard-earned capital returns and salary in order to pay the undeserving poor?

The definition of unearned income does not admit of "hard-earned capital returns." Banks talk about making your money "work" for you, but money doesn't work; people do.

Money accumulates more money without work.

As for the "undeserving poor," do you think the poor deserve their lot? With all of this unearned income in the economy? We hardly ever say the "undeserving rich," do we?

With $30,000, who will work? Won't we become a bunch of bums, beachcombers, and layabouts?

How about you? Would you not work at all? Or would you work more for the right reasons.

1. More income
2. Work is a good social scene
3. Work defines who you are
4. You don't want to be bored
5. You want to feel useful
6. You have projects you would like to do
7. Like art, writing, building a house, running a farm or a business

In order to place the stranger, you ask, "What do you do for a living?" With a shortage of workers (some of us won't work for a living, it is true), you will be able to demand interesting work. I think you would work, with the right conditions. And a $30,000 back-up cushion would allow you to demand the right conditions.

Number one on your list may be more income. It is for most of us. Honorable, interesting, satisfying work is the way to get more income. Sure, we will have more layabouts; not many.

Most of us are like you. Most rich people work. Of course they have a choice, as you will have. This begins to sound like freedom!

Honorable, interesting, and satisfying is fine. What about the difficult, dangerous, hot, cold, smelly, dirty tasks? Don't we all want to be sweet, clean, and safe?

You can be sweet, clean, and safe. Plenty of people are ready to be hot, cold, dirty, in danger, and smelly—for a lot of money.

The price will go up for those jobs. When the price goes up, employers will automate.

Prospecting comes to mind. The hardship and frost-bite and high probability of being murdered in this strenuous task should be rewarded. Most of such work can be done by mapping and machines and calculations. The romance and machismo of the rest can be paid for out of the proceeds, if any, with a generous salary and inducement for risk.

Claims may be staked, but excess income from the generosity of the earth will be taken to support all of her children; $30,000 is a generous grub-stake. We should let the market do its job.

I can be excused for differing with you about the number of layabouts. If a lot of us don't work, pigs will come to breakfast, and the shelves will be empty. What if most of us think $30,000 is enough?

You aren't so different from the rest of us. Few of us won't work at all. As for stuff to buy, don't forget about automation. Lots of the boring work is already done by smart machines. More expensive workers will ensure more automation.

Service is people oriented. It is fun. So is volunteering, as is running a business. Building up a farm is a challenge; and you will have the money to do it.

All of these activities yield products and services. They are mostly counted in the GNP. Don't worry, there will be plenty to buy. We will still be awash in products.

Automation won't be a bad word anymore. You will own the machines. Opposition to the machine is grounded in the coercive mode of thinking. Unions and strikes can not do what a shortage of labor will make necessary.

Remember the parable of the wind and the sun. The wind couldn't make the man take off his coat, whereas the sun did it in a trice. Employers will have to offer you the carrot, if they haven't got the stick.

You can thumb your nose at the loss of a job. You will be getting most of the return from that capital.

If I am getting most of the return from that capital, who will invest it? Doesn't it take rich people to make the investments that produce the jobs we need for a healthy economy? Why will they invest if they can't get all of the return?

You will invest it. You will be rich by your present standards. You will put away savings

1. for that rainy day
2. for your old age
3. for your hospital stay
4. for travel
5. for the kids' college educations
6. in order to buy a house

You will save just as the rich do now, perhaps even more than they do now. You will own the companies through your stocks and bonds. You will own the banks (which will do the investing even if you fail to do it). And you will profit as they make profit from the interest on their loans.

You will be able to invest in your own job, as workers do in cooperatives. There will be no shortage of investment funds (i.e., capital on which to run the economy) *if* we put some of the returns into your hands rather than give them all to the present holders of the moneybags.

All people can call themselves rich under this program. But they will not be wasteful. Super-rich people waste bundles of money.

If everyone gets \$30,000 in unearned income, doesn't that mean that the "super-rich," as you call them, will suffer?

I don't believe anyone will "suffer" with \$30,000 of unearned income. But yes, wealthy people, who get much more than this from clipping coupons, or having their servants do it, will have their unearned incomes adjusted to \$30,000, just like everybody else.

Unearned income is a gift from the universe and from other people. Such gifts should be divided equally among all of us.

This means that we take away excess gifts from some of us, and give them equally to the rest of us. A fair formula. We call this "redistribution of income." We don't take away wealth.

What do you mean, you "don't take away wealth"? If the rich are forced to sell assets because they don't get more than \$30,000 no matter how much they own, isn't this "taking away wealth"? You list inheritance among your examples of unearned income. If you take this, aren't you "taking away wealth"?

No one will be forced to sell assets. You can hold them as long as you live. There are many reasons for holding assets, even if they yield you no more than \$30,000 per year.

1. They give you prestige
2. They are something to brag about

3. They help you "keep up with the Joneses"
4. They give you power
5. You can try to buy political office
6. You can buy three houses with them
7. You can travel extensively, in luxury
8. There are many more "advantages" you can think of if you want to live high on the hog

Your inheritance is wealth to you as long as you hold it.

When it passes from one generation to the next, it becomes income, and is shareable. From this generation forward, then, inheritance will be taxed and distributed as unearned income.

If you're giving away money to poor people, why do you neglect the children?

I think we have not neglected the children. You can argue to give equal money to each baby born if you think that is fair, and if it fits your other values. But every income program, including our present *laissez-faire,* is a population policy. A rational population policy would give each mother an amount equal to half of the adult entitlement (not a dirty word) for the first child up to age eighteen. At eighteen, that person becomes eligible for the adult amount.

It would give the mother half of that first child amount for the second child, and none for her children after that.

This would not impoverish the mother, or her children, no matter how many she chooses to have. It would also encourage her to cooperate in a rational population policy, which we desperately need. It would also encourage fathers to live with mothers. Family values.

A few questions that may occur to the reader

What are the steps we need to take in order to carry out the program?

1. Find out all about the program. (Read this book.)
2. Send a postcard to America Tomorrow Publishers at P. O. Box 2343, Santa Rosa, CA 95405, giving your name, address, and telephone number. You will instantly become a member of a loose organization designed to install a fair income in your state, these United States, and the world.
3. This organization will help with petitions, constitutional amendments, and political campaigns. It will publish a newsletter as necessary. We will consult each other on the best means forward, and encourage lively debate with the opposition.

What more do I need to know in order to read this book?

Nothing. You already know that 50 weeks x 40 hours = 2,000 hours in a work year. And that employment is not certain.

I retired at fifty-seven; Joe Dominguez[1] did it at thirty-two. We still work, not for money. Interest and dividends and rent are paid every hour of every day: 8,760 hours per year.

It is good to have a piece of that constant accumulation.

---

1. Author, with Vicki Robin, of *Your Money or Your Life,* New York, Viking-Penguin, 350 pages, hardbound, $20.

Chapter 2.
Returns from earth and community, or how to play the real estate game, or getting rich in spite of yourself

We finally abolished slavery

It took men and women a long time to recognize that we cannot legally and morally own a slave and do anything we want with another human being. It will take us less time (especially since it profits us more) to realize that we cannot legally and morally own land and do anything we want with it without recognizing everyone's rights in it. That is our next evolution.

We have a hint of this recognition when government, in the name of all of the people, exercises the right of eminent domain, and "condemns" individual property ownership for the public good.

Justification, if that be necessary

The earth was created eons ago. It consisted of rocks and air and water and ash. No soil. Soil took millions of years and life. It requires billions of organisms—per cubic foot. Humans came along late in the scheme, roamed the mountains, plains, and deserts in search of food and shelter. No one had a thought about owning land.

In the last few centuries we have fought each other for position, killed each other by conquest, put up fences, and bought and sold "our" property—in a civilized manner, of course.

Whose property?

Whose property? Calling it ours takes some gall. Some of us take it from the Creator (who dishes out the gold and silver and coal and oil and iron and jewels and soil and water in a random manner) as if it were ours to discover and keep from everyone else. We act as though we know the mind of God.

That takes anthropocentrism as well as gall. When we take property in fee simple and act as though we can do anything we want with it, this is truly arrogance.

Everyone has an interest in all of the property, every minute of the day and night, every day and year, regardless of prior acts of piracy and conquest and the laws we pass in order to maintain privilege.

Fee-simple ownership is not enough

Until now, you (and the rest of us) have been the victim of wrong thinking in the system, according to which you believe you have nothing more to pay because you own property in fee simple (i.e., outright). The correction of this thinking says you own the property, so far so good; you have paid something for it, which is viewed by the Great Landlord as your license to occupy that piece of land. You still owe rent for the privilege of using that property—a use tax, if you will.

The arithmetic confirms the fact that you owe rent that is unearned income on property you own in fee simple. If you paid rent on that estate instead of owning it, the rent paid consists of a management fee, taxes, insurance, maintenance, and interest on the money invested in the place. All of these elements except interest on the capital value are earned income or external expenses. Pure rent, that is, the interest without these expenses, is quintessential unearned income. The money you have not invested in this estate is available to earn interest or profit in other investments.

If rent is not paid, it must be imputed

As a potential investor in this property, you have the choice of owning or renting. If you choose to sink your money in ownership, you will receive personal satisfaction from the ownership equal to or greater than the money income you could have received from investing that money elsewhere. The facts that you have exclusive use and that no one can break your long-term occupancy only add to your income.

You have to pay for these satisfactions; there is no free lunch, or ownership, not even for landlords—in a fair distribution of income. The fact that we have gotten away without paying for these satisfactions and income from ownership for years and centuries does not in the least justify these practices as correct.

When we look at unearned income from the standpoint of participating in the rent owed on privately owned and occupied property, we will include rent whether it is paid to the landlord or imputed to the owner-occupier. The correction may reduce the amount you have to pay for ownership after this law takes effect. It may raise that figure as we recognize the true value of private ownership. That is a matter of adjustment in ownership rights, or wealth. It is not an income matter.

When we have $30,000 per year income in place, the market, as always, will determine our wealth. Property, as any investment, can go up or down in price. You took a risk when you bought a place on the planet. The Great Landlord, for whom we are all agents, can change the rules at any time. Agents (i.e., all of us), acting together politically, will change the rules of income from property.

What's the good of it?

There is something to be said for our system, besides the fact that so far it is cruel and nasty and gives most of its rewards to the powerful. That is that private ownership with price as high as the market can bear is an efficient way to distribute resources.

The use that can pay the highest price will get the resource, and this use is the one that we want the most.

That goes for everything, even land, which we regard as a resource—not sacred, not beautiful, nor belonging to the species that live in and on it, but as an item to be traded and sold to the highest bidder. You may have mixed feelings about the market. That's the way it is.

There is a down side to efficiency

The other side of this efficiency is that the income that some of us derive from holding and selling and renting this resource is given to a few rich and powerful people or their descendants. At the risk of offending the Creator, it is hard to believe that this is what a just God would have had in mind when people came along.

What do we think is fair?

Fairness is a human concept. (God sends rain on the just and the unjust.) In all fairness it must be conceded that the income that comes from land and resources, and from people gathering in various spots, a settling that raises prices and rents, must be divided equally among us all.

Conquest gives us no right to it. Conquest is illegal and immoral. Purchase for a song gives us no right to it. (Manhattan for $24 worth of beads? That was a steal, just like all capital gains.) Capital gains from the sale of land are stolen from those who by their presence and demand have raised the price and caused this gain.

No one can work for it. Land is there. Given by the Creator for us all. But some of us want some of these resources more than others. Very well, let those who want them pay. But the payment has to go to all of us. Equally. That is fairness. That is morality. That is efficiency.

How you can get rich through real estate

I will only give broad outlines, since the details are boring. You can find the details by reading other books or by talking to a lawyer or an accountant. Consult your friends.

Smart landlords always get rich

Now that we have established the rights of all in the given fruits of the earth, we will learn how to work the system in order to get what belongs to us.

The system is rigged to make the landlord rich. So we might as well learn how to use it. Then we will all be smart.

All of us can be landlords when we install $30,000. Then everyone can be wealthy. First, let us learn how to think like the rich.

Wealth is not income

We have to distinguish between wealth and income. Wealth consists of the assets we own. Assets yield the income that we spend or save. Income also derives from work; then it is earned. If we save income, that becomes wealth. We can count it and look at it and brag about it. *But we'd better not spend it.* (Capitalist folklore.)

We are millionaires if we have assets of a million dollars or more. (We don't have to wait until we have incomes of a million to join the millionaires' club.)

The folklore of capitalism

Spending wealth is a no-no. It destroys the base from which we gain unearned income. Spending down capital is only done by the profligate children of rich people, never by the rich themselves.

Medicaid requires you to get rid of most of your assets before you become eligible. The aim is to get you to use these assets in your health care before the State pitches in.

People don't *like* to spend down their capital, or wealth. So they lie about their wealth or give assets to their children. And engage in other shady practices.

Such is the folklore of capitalism. And this is the way we respond to it.

Next, buy a house

Suppose you want to own a house. You manage to get together $10,000 or $15,000 for a downpayment. Borrow from a friend or relative if you don't have it. Borrow the rest from the bank.

The banks want you to have a good credit rating, so you must have paid your previous debts and bills and have a steady income.

These requirements will knock out half of us already. They will be easy to meet with your $30,000 per year after we pass the Plan.

You are on your way

When you are settled with your mortgage, you are on your way to becoming rich. "By paying all that interest?" you protest.

Why, certainly. The capitalists get their cut for lending you money that isn't yours, and allowing you to get your foot on the ladder.

Subsidies to the rich

Don't forget the advantages of that mortgage as you start traveling the road to riches. Interest paid on your home debt, up to a million-dollar mortgage, is now deductible from your income for tax. What a gift to those who are getting rich!

And that mortgage payment, which is largely interest at first, becomes largely principal or capital toward the end. This gives you ownership or equity in the house. After thirty years of making mortgage payments, here is your house, on a platter. At the end you own it "free and clear."

You are well on your way to becoming a millionaire. Helped along by those who have to pay the taxes that you don't pay.

Especially by the poor, who are not on the road to wealth, and so haven't received a house subsidy.

All of that interest was tax deductible. Here is your house, a gift from the poor.

Buy another building, on time payments

You don't, of course, stop at home ownership on your way to wealth from real estate. You buy another building and you rent it out. Set the rents so the tenants pay the mortgage. This is easy to do after a year or so of meeting your mortgage payments on time because your credit rating is now excellent. Especially if you have saved $15,000 or $20,000 out of your $30,000 unearned income under the Plan.

Even if we don't have the Plan and you are able to acquire a few thousand more to add to your savings, and put a down payment on an apartment or office building. With others in a partnership if you need more capital. Even if you don't want to do the work of putting the deal together.

There are plenty of available partners around. And many who will take your money and run if you are not careful.

Depreciation—what a steal!

Commercial property is even more profitable than home ownership, because you get an additional large subsidy from the government in the form of a depreciation allowance.

The theory of depreciation is that buildings wear out or become obsolete. They need to be replaced every once in awhile.

(Unless they become historical monuments.) For some strange reason, this theory applies to commercial buildings or investments, but not to the home where you live. Perhaps you are thought to be amply rewarded by the security of home ownership, even if the roof and walls fall down around you.

At any rate, depreciation is considered an expense for income tax purposes. So it is in the interest of landlords to make it as high as possible, which tenants have to pay in rent. And to replace and refurbish their buildings as little as possible, since this costs them money—even though they have collected the money.

To be perfectly clear, landlords are allowed by the IRS to reduce the value of their buildings by 3 percent to 5 percent per year (a replacement cycle of 33 to 20 years). This is an expense charged against their rental income, which means they have to pay no income tax on that amount. This is, in fact, required by the IRS, which has its own reasons.

Depreciation just goes on . . . and on . . . and on

Another interesting thing about depreciation is that it is so little tied to buildings or other manufactures. (All capital items except land are subject to it.) Your building may be sold whether it is fully depreciated or not. And the new owner can begin an absolutely new cycle of depreciation, which is as long as if the thing had just been built.

Build your wealth on depreciation

This makes depreciation an enormously valuable tool for accumulating wealth. If a building worth a million dollars is depreciated by you as a new owner over thirty years (an often-used period), and you collect that money in the rent, and you pay no tax on it because the IRS allows and requires you to treat depreciation as an expense, then you have an annual $1,000,000 divided by 30 (= $33,333) to invest as you wish.

Even at 6 percent interest compounded annually, an investment of $33,333 each year will amount to $2,793,360 by the end of thirty years. At 8 percent, it will grow to $4,078,153. At any time along the way, you can swap that building (it doesn't have to be simultaneous or with a single other person) for another that will keep your wealth growing from depreciation payments as long as you keep breathing. And beyond that.

Besides, you will probably make further money on the sale, which will be soaked up, no tax, in the "swap." The anonymous person(s) on the other side of your swap do the same thing. They start a new cycle of depreciation on your old building as you start one on theirs. The buildings themselves continue on.

They turn out to be primarily gimmicks for making money—money machines, or cash cows.

There are expenses

Of course, it isn't all gravy. While you've been piling up $3 or $4 million on account of depreciation, collected, untaxed, and not paid out, you have been paying out $72,650 per year (decreasing simple interest, which also includes principal payments), which equals $2,179,500 in thirty years, on mortgage payments. And if you have used some of your depreciation receipts to renew or refurbish a decrepit building, you will have less net from depreciation.

But this will be offset by an increase in the value of the building, which can now add *again* to depreciation.

But the bottom line is great

If you have kept the building through this cycle, you now have a $1 million or $2 million building, depending on how much improvement you have added to the building. (Maybe a $10,000,000 building, depending on inflation.) In addition, you have been collecting rent down through the years, which is a good bit more than depreciation.

28

Rent usually runs about 10 percent (per year) of the cost of the building. Taxes and insurance may run 2.25 percent. And the management fee you will pay yourself or someone else is about 1 percent of the building's cost. These percentages remain; but they result in increased dollar figures, as does the rent, when you upgrade the building, and when we have inflation.

Three to five percent inflation is now considered "normal." Double digits have been frequent in the past fifty years, much to the benefit of landlords.

This leaves you 3.75 percent to salt away, plus the management fee if you take it—at 6 percent or 8 percent interest per year compounded. Free and clear. You can have the fun of figuring out how rich you will be, at the expense of those of us who don't have the know-how or the gumption to get into the real estate game. It will be more than $5 million.

Save on the gain—or keep it all

There's more. If you have to divest because you have run out of depreciation (there is no value left to depreciate, and of course the building is still good) and you cannot find a comparable building to buy with your now increased capital, the capital gains tax is fixed at a lower rate than you as a rich person will otherwise pay on income. You save even on the gain.

If you swap the building for one that costs as much or more, you save all of the gain. The income keeps pouring in and the depreciation cycle starts all over again.

Warnings to the naïve

The usual warnings obtain. Don't pay more than ten times earnings or you're out on a limb hoping that inflation will catch up and rescue you from your folly. Don't invest in a place where the economy is on the skids and people are moving out. This might leave you holding an empty building. Realize that you are in a market where sharks operate; they have taken all of the good options and driven up prices in anticipation of inflation to the point where it is hard to find a property that returns ten percent per year of its cost.

So you have to be a shark, too. Look for the bargain in the cracks. Find a friendly real estate agent to comb the market for you. They are all friendly in search of the transient dollar.

Make even more by fixing it up

Take a fixer-upper, and do the work yourself. Years ago my wife and I bought a three-story house with a view of five counties and the bay for $10,500. It was riddled with rot and termites, not quite falling down. I poured twenty-two yards of concrete into new foundations under it, and did the appropriate reconstruction of mudsills and studs and stucco and bearing walls before leaving it as a home, renting it out for some years, then selling it, a sound building, for $150,000.

We are still living on income from it, having turned the sale price into a trust. I haven't pursued this as an occupation. There are more interesting things to do. And I already feel guilty enough.

Then put your assets in trust, and avoid taxes

By continuing to operate in real estate this way, using all of the government subsidies available, you can continue to get rich all the days of your life. And by cleverly putting your assets in trust, you can even pass your estate on to family and favorite charities without paying taxes on the bulk of it. Real estate, by the way, is only one of many tools by means of which the rich are able to gain their wealth without working or paying for it.

You may think I "worked" for that $140,000. We kid ourselves. I probably put another $10,000 into reconstruction, including my own time figured at $10 per hour, a princely wage at that time. The rest came off the gravy train.

Anyone can do it

Now that $30,000 per year is on the horizon for everyone, that sum will relieve anyone from guilt who builds an estate of a half million dollars, the amount that will yield that income forever at 6 percent interest. We can't get the guilt unless we exceed the income available to us all. We can even justify building a million dollar estate if we are ready to spend down capital on a long illness.

Thirty-thousand dollars in income, however, will go a long way toward paying for nursing home care. Of course we won't get the income beyond $30,000 unless medical expense requires it. By the time we need that, health insurance for all may be in place.

Did you steal it from the poor?

If you still don't believe that taking an unlimited amount of unearned income is stealing from the poor, please introduce yourself again to Henry George, who wrote *Progress and Poverty* a hundred years ago on this very subject. He is just as cogent and relevant today as he was then:

> The common right to land has everywhere been primarily recognized, and private ownership has nowhere grown up save as the result of usurpation. The primary and persistent perceptions of mankind are that all have an equal right to land, and the opinion that private property in land is necessary to society is but an offspring of ignorance that cannot look beyond its immediate surroundings—an idea of comparatively modern growth, as artificial and as baseless as that of the divine right of kings. . . .
>
> Historically, as ethically, private property in land is robbery. It nowhere springs from contract; it can nowhere be traced to perceptions of justice or expediency; it has everywhere had its birth in war and conquest, and in self-

ish use which the cunning have made of superstition and law. . . .

It is not merely a robbery in the past; it is robbery in the present—a robbery that deprives of their birthright the infants that are now coming into the world! Why should we hesitate about making short work of such a system? Because I was robbed yesterday, and the day before, and the day before that, is it any reason that I should suffer myself to be robbed today and tomorrow? any reason that I should conclude that the robber has acquired a vested right to rob me?

If the land belong to the people, why continue to permit landowners to take the rent, or compensate them in any manner for the loss of rent? It does not arise spontaneously from land; it is due to nothing that the landowners have done. It represents a value created by the whole community. . . .

Progress and poverty

George links poverty inevitably with "progress" and the private ownership of land. Hence the title of his book, *Progress and Poverty*. His writing is dramatic.

> Poverty is the Slough of Despond which Bunyan saw in his dream, and into which good books may be tossed forever without result. To make people industrious, prudent, skillful, and intelligent, they must be relieved from want. If you would have the slave show the virtues of the freeman, you must first make him free. . . .
>
> Does it [poverty] not spring from the existence of want? Carlyle somewhere says that poverty is the hell of which the modern Englishman is most afraid. And he is right. Poverty is the open-mouthed, relentless hell which

yawns beneath civilized society. And it is hell enough. . . .

Our primary social adjustment is a denial of justice. In allowing one man to own the land on which and from which other men must live, we have made them his bondsmen in a degree which increases as material progress goes on. . . .

It is this that turns the blessings of material progress into a curse. It is this that crowds human beings into noisome cellars and squalid tenement houses; that fills prisons and brothels; that goads men with want and consumes them with greed; that robs women of the grace and beauty of perfect womanhood; that takes from little children the joy and innocence of life's morning.[1]

French philosopher Henri Proudhon put it more succinctly in three words: "Property is theft."

Welfare is a pittance compared to our robbery from the poor of their birthright

Others besides Proudhon and George have been unkind enough to point out that our laws are means by which the rich steal from the poor. Anything we return to the poor by means of charity or welfare is a pittance compared to what we take. It is time we look at the larger aspects of this system in order to establish by logic the rules that will make it fair, or allow us to proceed without robbing "the least of these, my brethren," as Jesus spoke of the poor.

Logic gets a word in

We will take the sting out of this process by putting a limit on

1. Henry George, *Progress and Poverty,* first published in 1890, republished and kept in print by the Robert Schalkenbach Foundation, New York, 1955. Pp. 368-70, 406, 309-10, 457-8, and 548-50.

our take. This will make everyone equally rich from unearned income, part of which comes from the rental of property. If everyone winds up with the same amount of unearned income as everyone else, from whatever source, it becomes impossible for anyone to steal legally from anyone, let alone the poor.

We will divide up the rent, even on property we "own"

We need not apologize for dividing up the rent; nor for charging rent on property that is already owned. This will not disturb the people who enjoy the rights of possession and exclusive use, and it will not even take money away from 95 percent of us. The other five percent will feel better as their income from property is reduced to $30,000 per year because they will no longer be stealing from the poor the amount they collect above that magic figure.

Back to the practical

"But," I hear your protest again, "if everyone gets the same amount regardless of whether they go through the grief of managing their money or not, why should I do it? Why should anybody do it? And then why would it get done? And if nobody paid any rent because there wasn't any management, where would your system be then?"

No management, no rent, no gain, no system

Not so fast, my friend. Remember that you're playing the game. And there's fun to be had in the game. I know a fellow who's been playing this game all his life, to the point where he doesn't have to worry about how much money he makes. But he loves it. And there's a particular type of development he loves to do more than any other—for esthetic reasons. He'll keep on, and there are others like him.

People work for earned income

But there are more substantial reasons why the game will go on. The income one gets out of developing and managing real estate is *earned income*, which is subject to a different rule, not equality. Lots of people, perhaps all of us, will work for income; work makes it "earned."

If you don't trust the government . . .

The third reason, one that appeals to many of us, is that we are in control of our own assets that yield this unearned income. No one will take it away from us. No one will embezzle it at the federal level. If we don't have faith in the government to do its bureaucratic best, and we're afraid of "giving the government too much power," we'll still be secure. And while we're building up to those transfer payments beyond the $30,000 income that is ours to keep, and which others will depend on, we'll be safe with our nest egg.

This is a psychological argument, with little basis in fact, but it appeals to a lot of us.

You mean I am the landlord's agent?

As an owner of property under the new dispensation, you have two hats. You are the agent of the landlord, distributing the rent, and you are the tenant, paying the rent. You don't do one thing more than you do now as the owner of property. Right now, you are responsible for management (however little you do of it), maintenance, taxes, insurance, depreciation, and interest on the mortgage. As tenant, you have to pay the rent.

You will also be responsible as owner and tenant to fill out the form and pay your income tax. The activity is the same.

Your income tax will be different (we will all use the long form, and most of us will receive a refund), and the major work of preparing, as now, will be done by the form.

The total we have to work with

We need to estimate the national unearned income that will be produced by rent, in order to find out if this component added to the others will truly result in unearned income for each of us of $30,000 per year.

We also need to get some idea of the amount and kind of income transfer that will have to be done on account of rent.

The national income figures are rigged

Rent in the national income figures is given as income of persons in the amount of *minus* $12.9 billion in 1990.[2] This ridiculous figure is utterly useless for our purposes. It does not include the rental income or expenditures of corporations, it subtracts all expenses including depreciation, it includes no rent on owner-occupied properties, it allows property income to escape taxation, and therefore accounting, by step-up provisions in the law that allow unlimited capital gain between generations with no public accounting through living trusts. And it establishes the values of properties by tax assessments at less than market values, which gives landlords and owners additional advantages. That's how national income analysts convert billions of dollars of rent into a minus figure.

Other fine loopholes

The income tax law also allows owners to charge off interest paid on mortgages and depreciation as expense while "owners" are building equities in "their" properties. There are other fine loopholes that beg private persons to benefit at the public expense, to swill at the public trough, to steal from the poor.

If you don't know how to take advantage of them, you haven't hired a lawyer lately.

2. Statistical Abstracts of the U.S., 1992, p. 432.

We will find our estimate for total rental income through other means than the national income figures.

The Great Landlord collects; we are agents

Total rent collectible by the Great Landlord is found in three main areas:

1. private dwellings
2. commercial land, buildings and farms, and
3. royalties on resources

There were 93 million households in the U.S.A. in 1990, for which we will estimate rent at an average of $450 per month.

Some of these people live in slums or on the street where they pay much less than that figure. Most of us live in modest houses and apartments that rent for more than this. A few of us live in million dollar digs that would rent for $5,000 per month and up.

Four hundred fifty dollars is probably a conservative figure, which has to be reduced by 20 percent expense to get the real or economic rent of $360 per month. This then multiplies out to a total real rent from dwellings of $400 billion per year.

Non-households yield at least as much

The rent from commercial land, factories, offices, and farms will easily double that amount, an estimate of $800 billion.

Royalties from resources can be set at any amount by taxation, and some resources will be priced at much higher than current rates when we achieve the national good sense to save a few of them for our descendants.

What we could do with higher taxes

If we set the price high enough for oil, for example, we might use less of it. If we taxed gasoline at $7 per gallon, and this reduced demand to half of what we now use, that would save some of the precious stuff for our grandchildren as well as provide $500 billion per year in revenue—more than the national deficit.

We will not estimate here a $7 gallon of gas, but less than half that, which is about what Europeans now pay. We will estimate an annual return from mineral and other resources at $500 billion per year. This can be achieved by a tax on nonrenewable resources sufficient so that no more than one-thousandth of proven resources shall be used in any one year, the proceeds of which shall be divided among countries that have adopted fair income-distribution principles, including resources from the sea and Antarctica.

A partial tax on royalties

We also have a return from human resources, even though we are reluctant to classify human beings along with other things the Creator provides us as resources. Corporations have no compunctions about classifying their personnel as human resources. But we are here reaching for something more than the ordinary laborer.

The human being is the inventing animal, and we even add humans to our list of resources by calling the payments for invention "royalties." This confusion in the terms "resources" and "royalties" leads us to treat the human creation of something new as a category of its own.

We will here add the income from human invention and creation to that which we derive from other resources provided by the Creator. That is, we will add that income after a certain point. We will assume that creation entails labor. So we will allow the amounts derived from invention, the writing of music and poetry and prose, the execution of art great or small, the ideas for brand new ways of doing things (if they are patentable and exploitable for income) to be paid as *earned income* out of the proceeds of these new things up to the point where inventors receive the same amounts that others of their kind receive under contract.

Corporations provide the benchmark

This is easy to determine in the market for inventions. Corporations hire engineers to invent for them every day, and pay them excellent salaries. The individual inventor of similar stuff, if his or her royalties exceed the amount that would be paid by the corporation, will concede that the excess comes from the resource of which he or she is the carrier, and will no doubt be glad to transfer that excess to the rest of us as equal receivers for unearned income.

Artists and writers and dancers and champions and those who conceive great and original ideas will perhaps be perceived as laborers mainly, and will be allowed to receive the top salaries of their professions before they hand over the excess as unearned income. We will estimate the total unearned income from creation and fame of all kinds at $100 billion.

Total rent is $1,800 billion

Thus we arrive at the total economic rent of $1,800 billion per year. If this is spread around among us equally, this would provide each citizen with an annual income of $7,250. This is more by a third than the average rent we have assumed all homeowners pay. It is an even greater subsidy of tenants only. So we can assume that there will be a transfer of unearned income *to* more than 90 percent of us on account of rent alone.

All of us can welcome these transfers, which will allow us to live well in addition to making us rich.

Benefits beyond individual wealth

Millions of people would like to live in communities of their choice. Millions more see the cities we have as places where community is difficult or impossible. Children cannot grow up even safely, let alone healthy and well educated. The suburbs, to which the upper middle class has fled in pursuit of the American dream, turn out to be ghettos of single family loneliness, dependent on twin addictions: the automobile and TV. These are unsatisfactory substitutes for the crime, drugs, and squalor of the inner cities.

Rebuild cities as communities

Can we rebuild the cities as communities? Of course we can, with money and the will. $30,000 per year per citizen will provide the money. Who has the will and the imagination? Twenty families, your acquaintances and friends, can easily put together $800,000 each year in order to buy and rebuild neighborhoods that will live up to their name. Three years should suffice, then, before each family embarks on its own journey toward building wealth.

Patterns exist already. In Davis, California, a developer who later became mayor built such a community in the heart of town, and the houses have tripled in value because so many people want to live there. You can find many more in the publications of gifted architects.[3]

And amber waves of grain

Intentional housing and farming cooperatives will be greatly enabled by the national dividend. Thousands of people yearn to live near their chosen friends in cooperative agriculture. They are now prevented from doing so by lack of income and savings with which to approach a land and housing market that is beleaguered by inflated values.

I was recently approached by one of a group of Stanford graduates and students who want to put together a community of a hundred people on a thousand acres, which will be financially difficult even for Stanford people. Young people are idealistic, and may not realize the work ahead of them, but they are intelligent.

3. See, for example, Alexander, C., et al., "A Pattern Language," Oxford University Press, New York, 1977, 1171 p.

This particular call came from one getting a graduate degree in agroecology. Such calls come to Monan's Rill, the cooperative community where I live, about three times a month. They are no doubt repeated all over the country.

How to finance a community

If ten families organize themselves and want to buy land or housing together and make an average of $30,000 per family from work plus their national dividend income of $80,000+, they can put together a down payment of $700,000 from one year's savings. Monan's Rill land, bought twenty years ago of course, cost us $160,000 for four hundred acres near a medium-sized city in northern California.

With the national dividend, any group can enjoy the advantages of community, urban or rural.

$30,000 per person will save agriculture

We need a major overhaul of our agriculture in this country. Small farms and people are losing out at a tremendous rate to big farms and corporations. The technology is directed toward big machines, big fields, big capital investment that can take big losses as well as make large profits. Our agriculture is characterized by government subsidies, fertilizers and pesticides, monoculture, genetic engineering, millions of tons of soil blowing away each year and washing down the rivers—in other words, it is unsustainable.

The big turnaround is long overdue, and there are no other signs of this on the horizon. The national dividend will provide the impetus and the opportunity to save agriculture.

There are plenty of people who will subsidize their own farming with their share of unearned income. They need not join cooperatives to do so. They will be able to overcome the financial advantage of the big corporations with this help.

If this were the only reason for installing $30,000 per year per citizen, it would be worthwhile to do so.

Local and international rights

Two more items require our attention in this chapter; one is local and the other is worldwide. The local is the assessment of the value of land and buildings. This would be done, as it now is, by local tax assessors, but they would all have to work to the same national standard, which means that they would assess at market value, and federal inspectors would check their performance. Rents in excess of unearned income limits would be part of each individual's federal income tax, to be redistributed to us all.

Local taxes could be levied as they are now, by local tax collectors, but the process would be more fair if the tax on property were federally collected and returned to the counties by population. This would put people on an equal basis for schools and infrastructure regardless of where they live.

Who owns the land beneath the sea?

So far in the history of humankind the law of the sea has been just like the law of the jungle, including piracy, whaling, and fishing. Piracy, hunting, and fishing have been reduced but not made equitable by international agreement. But now that minerals have been found on the ocean floor and oil beneath it, we have instituted the 200 mile "limit" on sovereignty over seas adjacent to coastline nations. We have devised methods for exploitation of the wealth we find beneath the sea.

The U.S.A. does not sign the Law of the Sea treaty because our corporations reserve the right to prospect the sea (and the land wherever the strength of our arms and diplomacy will open borders to them) anywhere in the world for mineral wealth.

When we learn equity, we will turn over all sea bed exploration and exploitation to an international authority, which will pay finders and development fees and convert the values found in and under the sea into income for all of the people of the earth.

The system under which we currently operate is an extension of piracy.

Summary

The system of private property under which we operate is brutal, exclusionary, and no doubt unjust in the sight of the Creator. We can remove these deficits while retaining many of the benefits of the system by charging market rent for every piece of property, owner-occupied or not, and redistributing the rental income equally.

This would result in income greater than most of us now pay for housing, make most of us rich, reclaim us from the law of the jungle on land and piracy at sea, and make our agriculture sustainable.

This will provide each citizen with an annual unearned income of $7,250 per year.

Chapter 3.
Profit and interest are unearned income

Profits and interest are sacred cornerstones in our building of the capitalistic economy. To suggest that they should be widely distributed is tantamount to heresy. Nevertheless, we commit this heresy because these items are unearned income, which is gross injustice when they are delivered into the hands of a few; because this gross injustice produces social disintegration, riots, unequal opportunity, the waste of human resources; and because it is unfair.

You protest

"But," I hear you protest, "profits are not unearned income. They are the reward for taking a risk. You have to work in order to investigate the enterprise, in order to reduce the risk. The more risk you take, the higher the profit has to be; and the greater is the possibility of loss. You can't afford to take risk unless you are rich. So we have to have the unequal distribution of profit so the rich make the investments to make the economy go."

Your argument is incorrect

Your argument appears to be air tight, but in fact, it fails. Profit is the residual, left over after all other expenses have been paid, including interest on the capital invested. It is most often the result of monopoly, where the share is garnered and maintained by miraculous advertising or by patent or fortunate location or ownership of a scarce resource or by political pull or by force. Even Adam Smith, the guru of capitalism who wrote *The Wealth of Nations* in 1776, recognized that there would be no profit in a truly competitive economy.

Investigation is work that yields income

The investigation you do in order to avoid fraud and incompetence is not a reward for risk-taking. It is legitimate work performed by bankers and investment companies and the managers of mutual funds. It is paid for in salaries. If you do it yourself, you can deduct it from profit as earned income expense.

Your assumption that only the rich can afford to take risk is disproved on its face by the fact that middle class people by the millions invest in mutual funds where the risk is spread. If you consider the facts, you will admit that profit is unearned income. That's all we're saying in this heresy. As such, it is subject to redistribution as is all other unearned income.

Interest is even more so

Interest is even more unearned than profit, since risk is reduced in bonds and loans, and interest is money paid for the use of surplus. Compound interest (interest paid on interest) would wreck the economy, if spread to all investments.

Will redistribution wreck the economy?

The more frightening, and equally baseless, argument of the rich is that the economy will collapse if they are not allowed to keep their wealth and income and let these grow forever.

Will the economy collapse?

The American economy is this great, wonderful production

machine, which churns out products by the carload and money by the stack.

Waste

Oh yes, there is waste. Garbage and poisons by the riverfull and by tons wafted into the air. But the waste we don't see is the very essence of the system: competition and freedom of entry. Production in anticipation of demand. Selling the mistakes which result in bankruptcy. The system is touted as the most efficient in the world. But its trials *and errors* give it a very bad grade in the handling of its fundamental asset: capital.

Not only does it waste capital in competition that results in no better product—just mine vs. yours—and thus the failure of the hindmost, or of the advertising campaign, or mis-estimation of the market. It also requires companies to concentrate on the short term, to steal from the common heritage, to degrade the environment, and to foist external costs onto the public.

In short, it is a bad system of production as well as of income distribution. Don't get me wrong. Communism (state capitalism) was undoubtedly worse. We have a long way to go before we devise a sustainable system of production.

We will improve the system

We will not try to devise a better system of production. Marx tried that and failed. We will offer suggestions to improve what we have; small changes, sometimes larger, that will cut down losses, retain choice, improve profits overall, lessen our impact on the environment, and impose no fundamental barriers to operation of the system we have. Along the way and as part of the project, we will prove that the economy will not collapse with the proposed redistribution of income.

Where will we find the capital?

One of our widely held beliefs about the system is that we have to stuff the rich with more money than they know what to do with in order to provide investment money for business. We couldn't be more wrong. Investment money for business comes from the person(s) who will run it, friends, the bank, and markets for the firm's paper: stocks and bonds

If the entrepreneur happens to have a rich friend, that will help. It will not be enough, usually, for several reasons. The wealthy don't like to be the only supporter of a new, small business. They have plenty of other opportunities. And new, small businesses have a habit of failing. So investors diversify their risks.

The entrepreneur has a preference

The entrepreneur, also, doesn't want to be under the control of one or a few persons who hold most of the stock. He or she will want to retain that control, which means that they will sell only limited amounts of ownership to others. They will find a large number of small investors and go to the banks, which advance operating capital and buy bonds (all secured, on machines, buildings, and inventory in process). Banks can also provide venture capital.

The larger the number of friendly investors, the less likely they are to take over control, and the less likely they are to be super rich. It would be better, in fact, if all of the entrepreneur's friends had capital to invest.

More capital will be available for investment

$30,000 per year per person will make it easier for small businesspersons to get started. And new jobs are provided mainly by small business. Old business is constantly automating, restructuring, merging, downsizing, laying off large numbers of workers and moving their plants to places where costs are less. We will not only increase the number of new businesses by installing $30,000; we will increase the number of jobs.

Despite our logic, fear persists

We fear that interference with the grossly unequal distribution of income we have will slow down or stop the system of production that is synonymous with capitalism and that brings us the cornucopia of goods and services we enjoy.

What is that distribution now? It is greatly skewed to the point where a very few get huge amounts of income, a fat middle class gets a good income, and a large and growing underclass lives in poverty, with many below the "poverty line."

Justification, again

The justification for this distribution goes like this: the rich are the source of investment, and therefore of jobs. Take away a significant amount of their income and investment will dry up, jobs will evaporate, spending will decline, and more jobs will be lost. Follows an unending spiral into depression and worse, even to the demise of the system. Everyone knows this argument. It is drummed into us by interested parties every day of the week. So, is it true?

Again, the argument is lacking

On the face of it, the argument is lacking. It is suspect immediately because it is advanced by those who have a selfish interest in the *status quo*. You never hear a poor person say, "Keep these people rich in order to maintain the system." Second, it is an inefficient use of resources to stuff some people with so much money that they must waste it, and have to look for places to put it in order to make more.

What happens when people get money?

They spend it on the necessities of life. Then they save for the future and for disaster, old age, education, and big ticket items like travel. There is no reason to suppose that if poor people get more income they will act any differently than the middle class, which, due to its numbers, saves more money than the rich.

Rich people save, too

Of course the rich save money. They can't help it. They invest it, too. But when they invest in houses that cost a million dollars or more, as is commonplace, one is forced to question whether or not that saving and investment are good for the country. Such houses raise the cost of construction and damage the environment.

Rich people also bid up the prices of stocks and art and gold. What does that do for the production of income and jobs?

Inflation hurts mostly the poor

Then there is a great super-structure of price inflation in this country that soaks up tremendous amounts of capital. Wealthy people don't get caught by inflation; in fact, they gain by it! Even old people who complain of "fixed incomes" often have substantial investments in stocks and bonds that grow at a faster rate than inflation.

The conclusion emerges that there may actually be more money available for useful investment with income redistribution from the rich to the middle class and the poor than there is now. The argument of the rich begins to look tattered.

Saving and investment

More saving and investment will happen as a great many more workers become owner-operators of their workplaces. And this will happen as the banks become more educated to cooperative ways, and more responsible for investing in industry, large and small. (See "Mondragon" below.)

Rich people are not the driving force in the economy, investing in business and providing jobs.

Entrepreneurs are the driving force

This is the function of entrepreneurs, innovators, managers, and creators of new ideas. These people see an opportunity, and they grab it. They will get the money they need, provide goods and services, make a profit, and, incidentally, create jobs as part of the process.

No one starts a business in order to create jobs. That idea is propaganda.

Of course a few wealthy people are entrepreneurs, and some entrepreneurs become rich. But these functions are separate in the economy. It is fortunate that this is so, or we would get little innovation, especially as riches descend through the family and entrepreneurship does not.

Many are the businesspeople who try to leave their empires to succeeding generations of family only to have those empires crumble in the hands of bungling children. "Shirtsleeves to shirtsleeves in three generations," goes the proverb. So smart businesspeople leave their money in trust to succeeding generations of family members and turn over management of their affairs to strangers.

Banks create money

Very rich people are not needed even now to provide the money for investment in the economy. The banks can take care of that. When a businessperson or a consumer or a home buyer signs a note to a bank for a loan, the bank puts the amount of money loaned into the borrower's account. It comes out of thin air and it is that simple. That's the way money is created in our system, and the same amount of money is destroyed when the loan is paid off.

The Federal Reserve system can put limits on the total amount the banks can lend, but in general they are responsive to the needs of the economy. The rich can sit on their money, spend it wildly, refuse to invest it, or put it in the mattress, and the system will go merrily on, borrowing and creating the money it needs for prosperity. There is no theoretical limit to the amount of money the banks and borrowers can create. Money is limited only by the needs of persons and corporations, legitimated by the judgment of the bankers that borrowers are credit-worthy and by the Central Bank's desire to curb inflation.

We do not need great wealth in the hands of a few individuals in order to fuel the present economy. We will need it even less when all individuals are well off.

Conclusion

We have now concluded, and even emphasized, that there will be no lack of money for investment in new, small business when we install $30,000 per year per citizen. In fact, opportunities for such investment and the wherewithal will be greatly increased, thereby improving the health of the economy by providing more jobs than we now do, and thus eliminating most of the unemployment that is now chronic throughout the land.

A pregnant suggestion

We need now to look at a suggestion that has been lying on our doorstep for thirty years that will vastly improve the efficiency of capital by practically eliminating the need for firms to go bankrupt. In order to get the flavor of this suggestion, we will tell briefly the story of Mondragon.

What in the world is Mondragon?

When the cooperative movement was started by the citizens of Toad Lane, London, in 1844, according to ten principles which included equal participation, one vote per person instead of one vote per share of stock, patronage dividends of the profits according to the amounts that customers traded, and a fixed return to capital, these worthies did not confine their ideals to trade. Industry was just as much their target. So they set up a mill and made cloth.

When hard times hit the clothing industries in England a few years later, swooping capitalists, taking advantage of the co-op's short term losses, bought them out and thereby suppressed this "dangerous" form of competition.

The contribution of the Webbs

Some time later, Sydney and Beatrice Webb became the spokespersons of the burgeoning cooperative movement. They took their lesson from this failure, and concluded that co-ops could never succeed in industry. As a result, industrial cooperation became moribund for a hundred years.

Mondragon reversed this failure

"Mondragon" is a code word among students of cooperatives that stands for a remarkable group of manufacturing, trade, and banking businesses developed in northwestern Spain during the past sixty years. It is also the name of the small city where the first of these enterprises began as a vision in the mind of the local Catholic priest, Father José Maria Arizmendi. Father Arizmendi did not believe the Webb propaganda, based as it was on one failure. He added a couple of new provisions to the code, and conducted education in cooperative principles and behavior as his first contribution to the effort.

Some of the men who were not permitted any say in the management of the local iron works, and whose conditions of work were abysmal, took those classes and the principles to heart. They organized their own manufacture, at that time of paraffin-burning cook stoves, which they sold all over Europe.

52

The Caja Laboral

Not long after this successful enterprise was launched, the good Father saw a further need, and conceived a means to meet it. He called the men together and said they would have to start a bank. They were dumbfounded. They had no experience or training in running a bank—they were engineers and production spe cialists. And they objected

Nevertheless, they started a bank, called the Caja Laboral. And it, too, became tremendously successful. This was the means, marshalling the savings of the community, whereby new coopera tive enterprise could be funded.

A bank with a difference

But this bank contained in its charter and mode of doing business a fundamental difference from the others. It would over-see the businesses to which it loaned money. The bank set up a research department and asssigned a mentor, the "godfather," to each group of five or more persons who came to it with a good idea. Two years later, based on a careful study of production and marketing, a prospectus would be issued on each such business idea, on which a loan could be made and would be expected to be paid off.

The bank's responsibility does not end there. The mentor continues his oversight, and if the enterprise needs more money because of unforseen difficulties, the bank increases the loan, often at *less* interest, until the business is on its feet. The loan is always paid off, and the bank makes out handsomely. The Caja Laboral lights a candle down the dark road of the future. And it is as capi-talistic as the Bank of America.

The final nail

The argument of the wealthy that it is necessary that they be stuffed with money in order to provide the wherewithal for new business and jobs requires a decent burial. We have seen this argument as specious because it proceeds from self interest. We have seen also that the rich, in general, do not provide the business leadership that creates new products, opportunities, and jobs. Then we have seen that money is created on demand by the banks in the capitalist system regardless of what the rich do with their wealth. Finally, we have the example of the Caja Laboral, which oversees its investments and loans money in such a way that there are no failures.

Loans are paid off, and business succeeds in Mondragon, as opposed to up to 90 percent failure in some lines of business in America. We may have to change the rules slightly as we improve the efficiency of capital in our system, making the banks participate more in equity capital and in oversight of their investments. But success will follow our wisdom, *not* failure of the system.

Can we replicate the Caja Laboral?

We can require all banks to operate with research and oversight just the way the Caja does. And we can make them more friendly to cooperatives by requiring that they apply the same research and oversight to cooperative manufacture and marketing that they do to the standard model. Any discrimination would subject them to possible loss of their charter.

We need not be concerned that redistribution of dividends will affect the performance of established corporations. Corporations are not concerned over who gets how much of the dividends they disburse, or the number of their stockholders.

Pay out the profits

We have another suggestion, however, that will affect corporations more, and that will greatly improve the efficiency of capital: new laws that require them to pay out 90 percent of their profits as dividends. This would subject their decisions on expansion to the banks or the market for funds, which would improve their decisions. A second opinion is always desirable. We would want to balance this requirement against the desirability of allowing new, small business to grow in the difficult conditions of expanding a new market or competing in an old one. We would therefore suggest that the rule be imposed only after a business has been established for five years. This would help level the playing field between old and new businesses, and between standard corporations and cooperatives. Cooperatives hire capital at fixed rates, and all income derived from cooperative enterprise is paid out as dividends. Cooperatives always seek their capital from members and the banks. They may ask members to put their dividends back into investment, but the choice is explicit. The enterprise is always subject to the second opinion. (When cooperatives fail, of course, investors take the loss, as in any other capitalistic business.)

We have thus far considered that venture capital is the hallmark of capitalism. We will not disable it, and will even make it more efficient by the imposition of income redistribution. Another hallmark that is almost as distinguishing and that must be converted from a burden into an advantage is the interest that is paid and received in the economy.

Interest vilified

Human beings have for centuries declaimed against the evils of interest. They look at loans for thirty or more years and find that they as borrowers have to pay back more than the amount of the original loan in interest. They look at compound interest and see mountains of money stacked up as the result of the investment of a small amount for a century. They look at the national debt, which imposes an impossible burden on our children and our children's children that will never be paid off. It will result in inflation that will ruin them. The interest alone will cripple all future generations.

The Christian church in the Middle Ages imposed edicts against usury, which forced the profitable business of money-lending on the Jews. The Muslim religion still forbids lending at interest. The State of California has a usury law on its books, which is honored more in the breach than in compliance.

A redeeming social benefit

All of these complaints against the levying and collecting of interest are half right. Interest has at least one positive and useful function. It allocates scarce resources among competing uses. It ensures that only those enterprises that can pay this freight will receive the money to begin, build, and expand.

It requires a distinction between present gratification and future benefit. It forces us to think when we pay our credit card bills. It provides a brake on consumption. It ensures that anyone who has a good case and credit can get cash. It dispenses with favoritism in lending and imposes caution in spending. It is an elegant underpinning for democracy.

Loans are a source of money for the running of business almost as important as venture capital itself. The government could hardly keep order in the streets without the possibility of borrowing money. We will not be guilty of throwing out this baby with the bath.

Interest will be no burden

As for the burden of interest; that is well described at present as another of the tools whereby wealth and income are transferred *from* the poor *to* the rich. Assuming that the rich know what they are doing and the poor are less informed, it is another form of stealing. When $30,000 per person is installed, this effect of interest will no longer obtain. Franklin Roosevelt's dictum that it is no burden because "we owe it to ourselves" will be correct, not hyperbole.

Profit and interest are unearned income

Middle class people (there will be no other class) will invest in bonds, the interest from which (as well as profit and rent) will support their spending habits and their saving. Since all interest will be returned to all of us in the national dividend, it can't be a burden to any of us.

All interest goes into the national dividend

The treatment of interest as unearned income fulfills the definition (no one works for it), adds a benefit to the list, and removes all of the objections we have listed above—when we get our $30,000. You may continue to put down interest as a deductible expense on your home mortgage or in your business. It continues to allocate resources and provide an underpinning for democracy.

Everyone will receive interest income. The national debt will no longer burden us or our children, since the interest, which will be paid by all of us in fair taxes, will accrue to all of us in *fair income.* You will always have enough income to pay the interest on your mortgage, which will be a small part of your *national dividend.* If we see the interest question whole, and treat it as unearned income, we will welcome interest, not complain about it.

What will we do with all that money?

The question that will occur to bankers and brokers and investment counselors and managers of mutual funds is, "What will happen to all of the savings?" Economists will wonder, "Will the total of savings and investment be increased or reduced?" These are all aspects of the same question.

Not much will happen

My conclusion is that not much will happen to the overall parameters. This is *redistribution,* not an increase or a decrease in the pie. Even within the categories, present trends will continue. More money will continue to flow into mutual funds. Bonds will continue to be bought and sold. If we enforce the improvements to make capital more efficient, we will become even more affluent than we now are. Cooperation will become a more important element in the industrial framework.

Avoid speculation

My friends Joe Dominguez and Vicki Robin[1] recommend that you avoid speculation by investing any surplus you have in government bonds paying 5 percent or 6 percent more or less. Eliminate the middleman and the expert, do it yourself, and let the government pay you the interest on the national debt. Your capital will not grow enormously, but neither will you lose it. And of course, you will not speculate on margin.

Whatever you do with your excess, we will assume that it is possible for you to achieve 6 percent to 8 percent per year, compounded, of profit (dividends + capital gains) and interest on your investments. Under the plan for redistribution that gives you a $30,000 per year income from all investments, and if you can live on your income from work plus save, say $5,000 on that score, we will assume that while you are working, at least, you and your spouse can save $75,000 per year. This is probably more than you now save.

$75,000 per year at 6 percent compounded will give you a capital base of $550,000 in about six years. Presumably you could do this several times over in your working life. Or you could retire before age thirty and do good works, build your dream house, travel, enter politics, create art, home-school your children, take care of the aged, or do whatever gives meaning to your life.

---

1. Op. cit. Joe is a former stockbroker who recommends that you live frugally and retire early.

What about new businesses?

In a new business, the owner-manager typically works long hours and takes as little salary as possible in order to put profits back into the enterprise and make it grow. He or she hopes to make a fortune in five or ten years by making the business large and selling it, or creating a joint stock enterprise, the shares of which rise in value to a multiple of the original offering price.

Here comes unearned income

When it comes to getting rich by selling the business or retiring on the increase in the value of the stock, we are into unearned income. The earned income in this deal has been compensated by salary. Again, equality in unearned income would allow that the seller may receive an amount that is up to seventeen times $30,000.

If the owner prefers to hold stock in the company in order to retain some control of the business, he or she will be limited in the receipt of dividends to the $30,000 that others receive in unearned income. If it is invested in other assets that yield 6 percent, this would diversify the seller's portfolio and eliminate the control of management. If the seller does not invest the proceeds in any assets that yield 6 percent, the receipt of gain would be counted as unearned income and limited to the amount that others receive from unearned income.

The national dividend

It is easy to see at this point that the amount we all receive of unearned income from the economy should be called the national dividend. This is received from our own investments or derived from the excess unearned income of others. It can be estimated each year by the General Accounting Office, and adjusted more frequently by changes in the price index. The limit we have arrived at, $30,000, adjusted by the more accurate efforts of national accounting, will be used by the Internal Revenue Service as the standard against which to tax and transfer among those of us who receive more and less.

What will happen in the stock market?

We can speculate on what will happen, but the market always takes care of itself. That's its nature and its charm. We may be surprised. The holder of millions of shares worth billions of dollars may not find it worthwhile to spend time speculating in the hope of making more millions of dollars, since that hope now comes up against the standard. That holder may wish to sell. Who will buy? The owners and savers of new millions of dollars in the new middle class. Stock prices may move up or down, but it is unlikely that they will crash.

What about the funds?

Pension funds, welfare funds, insurance companies, banks, mutual funds, and other large institutional holders of stocks will find one source of their incomes severely limited when they have to pay out the interest, rent, and profits they receive. This means that insurers will pay out what they take in from premium payers. Not more. Their clients cannot expect to benefit from stock market speculation. Investment companies will be little affected.

How much will there be?

How much does the total of profit and interest add to the national dividend? Corporate profits reported by the Census Bureau for 1990[2] were $362 billion on a total income of about $11 trillion. Proprietor's income from small and unincorporated business is given as $367 billion, half of which we estimate as labor income. The other half is non-taxable profit for the first five years.

2. Statistical Abstracts of the U.S., 1993, Tables 697 and 848.

Tighten the rules

It is common knowledge that corporations charge to expense, and thus reduce income, large amounts that some would argue are not necessary to production, such as money spent for chauffeured automobiles, company airplanes, business luncheons and entertainment, tours and guests, political contributions, etc. If we can tighten the rules on deductions, we may well add $100 billion to profits on this score.

Our old friend depreciation also appears here as "consumption of capital," for which the amount given was $368 billion in 1990. At least half of that figure is "accelerated" (i.e., charged to expense in less than three years after installation). A realistic figure for depreciation actually expended would perhaps be two-thirds of $368 billion, or $245 billion, leaving $123 billion of that expense in profit. Adding these residuals, we come up with an actual profit estimate of $695 billion available for distribution to us all.

So much for profit; what about interest?

Interest is given in the national income figures as $460 billion paid by corporations. Interest received by business in 1990 was approximately $500 billion. Personal interest income was $695 billion. These figures are given as "net." Crunching these numbers and estimating a $200 billion loss from double counting rounds the interest figure from all sources to $1,455 billion.

Adding our estimates for profit and interest gives a total of $2,150 billion, which, when divided by the 1990 population of 248 million, suggests that profits and interest will contribute approximately $8,670 for each citizen from the unearned income pool.

Summary

We commit the ultimate heresy by suggesting that profit and interest, the hallmarks of capitalism along with rent, are also unearned income. As such, they are subject to redistribution above unearned incomes in the amount of $30,000 per year.

The argument of rich people that we must maintain high salaries and income in the hands of a few people in order to keep the economy from collapsing fails on four counts: it is a self-serving argument; it is a wasteful method of financing industry and growth; rich people are seldom the entrepreneurs who put deals together and build new businesses; and the banks can supply all of the money the economy needs regardless of what the rich do with their money.

Far from making the economy collapse, the redistribution of interest and profit in the economy beyond a total of $30,000 per year per person from unearned income, along with a few other suggestions for increasing the efficiency of capital, will strengthen the economy, reduce unemployment, and increase the national income.

The limit on unearned income will keep any of us from getting *very* rich. We have found that *very* rich people are not necessary to the economy. The trade-off is income security for all. No matter where we go or what we do, we will have an income that is sufficient to maintain us in comfort, not luxury, that will maintain us in sickness and in health, from the day we are born until the day we die. Our financial anxiety for the future will vanish.

It is almost better than getting married to a wealthy person. It doesn't keep us from getting married; we will all be "wealthy" in our own right; and we can't be divorced from it. The contribution of profit and interest to our equal unearned income will be $8,670 per citizen per year.

Chapter 4.
Payment for human-made products and services

Workers with hand and brain will get smart with income redistribution. We will join the twentieth century before it becomes the twenty-first. Our present orientation is stuck in the battle, which we are losing every day. We are tired of losing. Organization, demands, and strikes are the tired old ways of losing.

Modernization, downsizing, moving the plant—these are the tools of the capitalists. We will *use these tools* to stabilize our incomes, to maintain our homes, jobs, and communities, to get our share of the American dream, of the total income pie. We will use these tools to own American industry. All of us. And we will win.

A capitalistic economy

We are a capitalistic economy. So our income derives largely from the use of capital. More of it every day. As owners of the capital, which we will become with $30,000 unearned income, we will take that share as other owners do—from dividends, interest, and rent.

Income from the work we do will become a smaller share of our total income, and we will be better off. With this distribution of our income, unemployment will not be a catastrophe, and homelessness will not be a possibility. Our workplaces can be sold, moved, or closed, and we will not starve or be homeless. We will be owners of the whole economy.

We will examine work

Just as we have for those twin pillars of the economy, profit and interest, we will examine wages and salaries to determine the effect on all of us of some redistribution in this area. We will begin with workers, graduate to executives and superstars, continue with proprietors, developers, prospectors, inventors, and entrepreneurs, and conclude with the amount we can expect to be added to unearned income for all of us from this sector.

Some wages will be converted to capital returns

We workers have been fighting the battles of the nineteenth century, the battles of Marx and Engels, in an effort to raise our wages by negotiations with and strikes against owners and management. We are losing at every turn as strikes are broken, laws are passed restricting organizing, automation is installed, plants are moved, and unions are weakened.

This is not a temporary phenomenon. It is a losing fight. This is happening because we are becoming a more highly capitalized economy every day, and capital is becoming more flexible and mobile. We should be aware that 90 percent and more of production is the result of tools, machines, techniques, and energy not supplied by current labor.

Automation is here

Automation, despite labor's desperate rearguard action, is here today, and will be here tomorrow. Jobs are being lost to machines and smart management all over the landscape. John Scully, the chief executive officer of Apple Computer Company until recently, reported on January 28, 1987, that the company's new MacIntosh factory, located in Fremont, California, is so fully automated that direct labor is only *one percent* of the cost of the product! And the labor that is employed only maintains the machines. One percent is $10 per thousand dollars of product cost.

The point of this example is that we, the workers, in a large number of cases, produce a minuscule amount of the product that labor and the machinery of our world pour out. If IBM and Chrysler and General Motors don't downsize and restructure and automate and lay off thousands of workers and move plants to Mexico and Singapore and Taiwan today, they are out of business tomorrow. We workers flail in vain at these facts of our existence.

All of us have to be capitalists

Before the unions are completely smashed[1], it is imperative that we, and all of labor, undertake a change in strategy. We must recognize that much if not most of our income derives from the use of capital, and we will go after it as capitalists or we will lose it.

The workers' standard of living in this wealthiest country in the world has dropped by more than 10 percent in the last ten years, because we are thinking in terms of the last century and before while jobs are moving abroad to cheaper labor pools. The technology of the present is engulfing us!

When plants are moved abroad to areas of low wages, workers are not supplanted job for job. Those new plants are built with the latest technology, and ten jobs may be lost here for every six gained in the third world.[2] But these statistics don't impress us. Statistics do not put bread on the table.

---

1. See Geoghegan, Thomas, "Which Side Are You On? Trying to be for Labor When It's Flat on Its Back," New York, Farrar, Straus, and Giroux, 1991.
2. See "Your New Global Work Force," by Brian O'Reilly, *Fortune,* December 14, 1992, p. 52.

From management's point of view, machines are always preferable to workers. Machines don't organize, don't strike, don't demand health benefits, lunch rooms, toilets, clean air, good light, or old age pensions. When they wear out, or are superseded by newer technology, they are junked. And costly retraining is avoided while profits from capital soar.

We are becoming more capitalistic

It may be difficult to admit that labor, which is becoming more and more of an adjunct to capital, receives unearned income; that labor's income should be divided differently from the way it has "always" been, and that labor should get part of its return from the capital with which it works in the production of joint products. But life is difficult. We shall have to change our minds.

Labor's income is typically seen as all earned income because it is so termed in the tax returns, we have "always" thought of it that way, because economists and politicians say so, and because Marx enshrined labor as the only legitimate receiver of income in his Labor Theory of Value. We are more indebted to Marx for our thinking than many of us would like to believe.

However, candor will convince us that labor has indeed much unearned income, and that the laborer's income is not a special case. Some of it should be recognized as what it is, a return from capital. It should be received as a return on capital (profit and interest), and it should be shared with all of us, just like profit and interest. Labor will be better off, not worse. Labor will get what it deserves by political means, without a fight.

Hence a guaranteed income

The only way workers will regain power and control over their lives and income is to participate in the distribution of the income from capital. Hence a guaranteed income, $30,000 per year from capital, that will restore workers to a position of power without slighting the disadvantaged. Power will accompany labor shortage, which will accompany income redistribution.

Five more advantages to the shift

There are more advantages to shifting some of labor's income to the income derived from the capital with which it produces. One is that now a large part of labor's production-based gains derives from organization into unions, demands, confrontation, and strikes. These often result in hard feelings and productivity slow-downs that run into years of bickering and bad relations—not the best atmosphere for cooperation in our joint enterprise. Conflict discourages responsibility and joy in the work. Distrust and bad feeling encourage featherbedding. This will all change.

Another is that the income from capital sticks with the owner; it is not income that moves with the job. Plants can go anywhere on earth, and workers as owners will benefit to the extent that they are paid profit. Management can automate to its heart's content, it can sell the business to another corporation that will restructure and downsize, and workers will feel little or no squeeze as they collect their unearned income while finding other, more satisfying opportunities for work.

Income will not be lost

A third advantage is that a great deal of income, which is the support of consumption and therefore of jobs and the economy, will not be lost when workers change jobs and are thrown out of work. Unemployment insurance and welfare have been recognized as a steadying influence on the economy ever since they were instituted in the Great Depression of the 1930s. $30,000 per year per person is a much larger lifeline, and it will sustain the economy to a much greater extent.

A fourth is that unemployment will become short and merciful and a welcomed chance at leisure as workers search for new jobs in a labor-short economy. The labor force will be smaller with a fair income because some people will become full-time parents, others will travel or take sabbaticals or re-train for mid-life career changes or retire early by choice, not by necessity.

A fifth advantage is that even at one percent of cost in a fully automated plant, the worker is necessary to the production. Without the worker, as without the machines, there would be nothing. With labor taking pay as capital return up to 90 percent of production cost, the economy would be extremely stable without further regulation. And we have the further regulation that will be possible at the point of transfer among owners of capital. This will have to take place through a government agency (i.e., the Internal Revenue Service) and we may call this place "The Fund."

So we calculate

The amount we calculate to be designated as the capital return out of wages is initially suggested at 60 percent. It should probably be higher, given the objective facts of the income derived from production. And the higher it is, the better off labor would be. But we are accustomed to taxes not far below this range, and we may wish to experiment with this figure to begin with.

As in the case of other unearned income, we will allow this unearned portion of wages to be retained in the worker's paycheck to the amount of unearned income that everyone receives, $30,000 per year. If workers have no other assets, they can receive up to $30,000 of wages and salaries per year as unearned income, which may equal 60 percent of wages before any of it is transferred.

The remaining 40 percent of earned income would be another $20,000, making a total of $50,000 per year, with no transfer of the unearned portion, and the total subject to the regular income tax. ("Regular" income taxes will be smaller than now, and the national budget will be balanced, because a great deal of income now in the hands of the rich will no longer escape taxation through loopholes.)

Therefore, most of us laborers and skilled craftspersons will see our paychecks increased. And unemployed people will also find that their share of unearned income continues.

Some Independent contractors will pay more tax

Doctors, dentists, lawyers, some accountants, and other independent contractors make from $100 per hour to $500 per hour. We will assume $150 for our example, which is an annual wage of $300,000 if such contractor works a normal year of 2,000 hours. (They may, indeed, work less by doing unpaid work or by taking time off which costs them $150 per hour in lost income.)

Clearly, independent contractors pay all of the costs of their benefits, and they knock on the ceiling of income tax, which we will assume to be 36 percent in this bracket. Their tax on $300,000 of income would therefore presently be 36 percent plus 18 percent benefits plus 8.5 percent when we install universal health insurance, or 62.5 percent on the total. This is a total tax and transfer of $187,500, leaving $112,500 net income under present circumstances modified by universal health insurance.

When we institute redistribution, this contractor will receive $180,000, 60 percent of his or her income as return on capital, which would result in a tax and transfer of unearned income in the amount of $150,000 ($180,000 minus the $30,000 allowed maximum for unearned income.) The remainder, $150,000, would be subject to the high bracket income tax of 36 percent, leaving a net of $96,000.

However, that amount is $17,000 more than the maximum salary allowed by the ten times rule (see below for the ten times rule), so $17,000 more would also be transferred to the Fund, leaving $79,000 net earned income. Earned and unearned income now total $109,000.

Voilà! The break-even point of gross income between the old and new systems is close to $300,000 of gross income, at which both would yield an after-tax income of $109,000 to $112,000.

Mondragon Cooperatives can inform us

The experience of the Mondragon Industrial Cooperatives offers guiding examples for executive salaries, for worker satisfaction, and for investment banking principles in starting new businesses. We can search their experience for more nuggets of information as we learn a more generous lifestyle.

As we develop more power to affect our industrial surroundings without the crude and brutal tools of confrontation and strike, and as we look around us for better models of work and play, Mondragon can indeed inform us.

The size of the difference

We are particularly interested in how much more we have to pay an executive than the lowest paid worker in the plant in order to call forth executive skill and responsibility. In the Mondragon industries, the factor is six. The top executives get six times as much as the lowest paid worker in the plant. At Scott Bader, the cooperative plastics manufacturer in England, the factor is seven. These companies exist in a capitalist world in which some executives get as much as ten thousand times the pay of the sweeper.

If the economy were structured in such a way that no top pay was more than ten times the wage of the lowest paid (including perquisites), then even Americans could feel satisfied with their salaries. This comes along with the security of an unearned income that doesn't stop, and allows comfort, not excess, to everyone including executives. It is likely that officers would continue to put out their best within this framework, as they do in cooperative industry.

Superstars and politicians

What about superstars and politicians and others who live on a gravy train that exceeds these modest limits? Will they still perform and want to run the country and play football and sing? They can, of course, receive any amount in gross salary to compare with others in their class. So their desire to compete can still receive the recognition it so richly deserves. If taxes curb their desires for excess consumption, this can only redound to the benefit of the environment.

Their desire is more a claim for fame than it is for money, and they will not perceive unfair treatment if everyone is subject to the same law. So stars will continue to shine, as they always have for fame, they will reap an additional benefit of feeling fair about their incomes, and they will enjoy an adequate continuing income for life even when they burn out.

But will workers continue to work?

If you can get an adequate income without working, why work? This question is asked by those who have been coerced to work all of their lives. It is an outgrowth of the Protestant work ethic, which proclaimed, in the provincial days of John Smith, that "He who does not work shall not eat." We still apply this thinking to everyone except the rich.

Some of us are particularly galled by welfare payments, which go to the "idle poor," and come out of the hides of those of us who have to work for a living. So we try to make everyone work, and this is very difficult in an economy that doesn't provide enough jobs.

Why do the rich work?

We get a glimpse into the workings of our minds by observing the present rich, who mostly work. Why do they do it? Partly to fulfill their lives. Partly to escape boredom. Partly to enjoy a social situation, which work is. Partly to engage in something meaning-ful and important. Partly to create something new.

Partly because their identity is wrapped up in their work. Ask a person who he or she is, and nine times out of ten they will answer, "A teacher; a plumber, a machinist, a minister," or some other name that is related to their work.

People also work partly in order to increase their incomes and pile up more wealth. Partly in order to show off a steady flow of super-consumption. Only the last two reasons have to do with income. And income reasons are the ones usually put at the bottom of the list in surveys of why workers work.

A few will refer to the Protestant work ethic by admitting they would feel guilty if they didn't. They have to give something back to a generous Universe in order to justify their existence. Many will say that their work is boring, but many also will say that it is interesting. You couldn't keep them away from it.

Good work to be done

So there is good work to be done. In a situation where money is clearly no longer a large reason why people work (which is already the situation and will become even more so), and people have the power to withhold their work if they don't like it, it is reasonable to infer that most work will become interesting and important.

Employers will have to make it so. Workers will demand interesting and important work. They will not refuse to work. We have already listed many reasons why we work. I suspect that almost all of us who can, will work. And that a great deal more joy will be manifested through our work than now exists.

More of the Mondragon experience can teach us

All of industrial life is cooperative. It has to be. Everything we do as a company engaged in production we do as a team, as an organization, as a group, as a whole. (Of course there are individual owners and producers who work with others only through their market connections, but we will leave those out for the present as we discuss the norm.)

It is the constant desire and task of management to elicit our cooperation, to make us joyful workers, enthusiastic, speedy, happy, productive, and super-efficient. Endless research goes into new ways to motivate us to produce more.

Management now realizes much more than it ever thought during the heyday of the industrial revolution that human beings are complicated bundles of wishes and desires, feelings and rationalization, rumor and belief, respect and resentment, love and hate, fairness and exploitation, humor and growls. We are much more interested in how we are treated than we are in strictly salary matters. And all of this reflects in the bottom line of the company.

Cooperation can't be coerced

The trouble with our present model is that cooperation is subject to coercion. It can rarely be voluntary and freely given. There is a built-in conflict of interest. If the employer gets one percent more of the pie, the employees get one percent less. All of the wishes and wants of the workers cost the stockholders money—except attitude. The Japanese realize that attention and attitude cost nothing, so the boss wears coveralls and eats in the cafeteria and parks in the common lot.

Coercion and cooperation mix about as well as oil and water, so in America, concessions have to be fought for, confrontation is the norm, and feelings of resentment often determine work pace and quality rather than pride in speed, output, and workmanship. The effect of true cooperation on the efficiency of capital is becoming more obvious.

Cooperation flourishes where owners and workers are one

No wonder the industrial cooperatives of Mondragon compete handily in the markets of the European Economic Community, as well as provide superior employee benefits, retirement plans, cheap groceries and housing, and other perks that cost money.

The employer and the employee are one. Middle management can be and is left out. Expensive oversight is unnecessary where the cooperation is voluntary, and savings, speed, and quality redound to the benefit of everyone. No one cheats where everyone watches, and Luddite tactics that hurt the bottom line of the employer, such as group slow-down and work-to-rule, are unknown.

Cooperators *are* the employer as well as the workers. Conflict of interest is gone. Strikes as a last resort to improve wages and conditions with their high costs in lost production and pay are no longer seen as the way to go. Suspicion and backbiting are replaced by friendliness and trust. Again, we would see in redistribution an improvement in the efficiency of our capitalistic system.

There will be a chronic labor shortage

The net results of all of this easing of the competitive scramble of our lives will be a shorter work life and fewer people in the labor force at any given time. We will probably turn around from a surplus labor economy to a situation of labor shortage. That's what we had during World War II.

From the standpoint of the employer, this will be unwelcome. It will mean higher wages in order to attract more of us out of our leisure. The employer's power over the worker will diminish. From the standpoint of the worker, it will be a dream come true. More jobs available than would-be workers in line for them. No more layoffs, firing at whim, evil and dangerous conditions of work.

Labor shortage will accomplish in weeks what the Occupational Safety and Health Administration has been unable to make employers do in years of badly enforced regulation. With a fair income, no one will be unemployed. There will be no unemployment insurance. There will be no bureaucracy to register and check up on unemployed people. No one will be around to see if you are cheating or looking for work.

People will be at leisure from time to time, between jobs, getting more education, traveling, taking time off, retiring early, and doing volunteer jobs.[3] Their unearned income will always be sufficient to take care of their needs.

Automation will boom

There will be much greater automation than we have now. Labor will no longer have reason to oppose automation, since it no longer throws workers out of jobs in a labor short economy. (Of course, it does that temporarily while they train for new jobs that give more satisfaction.) And with the profit from automation put into the Fund, labor as well as the rest of us will benefit with more unearned income in our pockets.

Hot, noisy, dangerous, smelly, dirty jobs will be taken over by robots, as people, now more independent and able to voice their wishes without fear of reprisal, refuse to perform this work. Any such jobs that our ingenious engineers cannot handle with smart machines will command very high wages indeed, and will always find macho daredevils to perform them. We may employ a national service contingent, and undocumented workers (an historical necessity) to harvest the crops.

Development will be less speculative

Developers typically attain a certain kind of vision, by which they can see a new use for a building or a piece of land, or a better

---

3. "An idle mind is the devil's workshop," goes the proverb. But whose mind will be idled by dull, repetitive, boring work in this cooperative economy?

place or plan of production, or how a large project like a railroad should be conducted in order to maximize profit. Then they promote these ideas, putting together the money from other investors as well, and if they are successful, they make large profits on their initiatives.

They are as subject to fads and groupthink as other investors, and often contribute to gullibility and failure as they overbuild or oversell their projects. They are on the speculative edge of doing new things. And they are everywhere that the lure of profit motivates human beings.

Would we continue to have development, say of housing projects, office buildings, factory complexes, industrial parks, freeways, airlines, dams, the information superhighway and other grand ideas in a capitalistic economy in which profits from such activities were capped?

Well, we have had the pre-capitalistic pyramids of Egypt and Mexico and the great cathedrals of Europe in the Middle Ages such as Chartres and Mont-St.-Michel, and the Taj Mahal in India and Angkhor Wat in Cambodia and the Great Wall in China. There must be other incentives than greed that call forth the most awesome achievements of the human mind, hand, and heart.

In fact, we don't have anything awesome to show for greed except destruction. Towering office buildings in our largest cities? Hardly awesome. An airplane? Not likely. The tunnel under the English Channel? No big deal. Space walk? Just an extension of our capable minds. And none of these are the works of individual developers.

The destruction of the rain forests in the tropics? The destruction of the hardwood forests in North America? The elimination of the passenger pigeon and practically the bison and the Native American? These may be awesome, but they do not invoke pride.

Cooperatives again

Again, we can turn to the cooperative movement for instruction on purposeful development in the capitalistic mode. In cooperatives, development takes place in response to need. Of course, individual developers try to anticipate need, or there would be no profit—except from speculation (and they don't mind speculation, so long as they get in and get out with their profit.)

In cooperatives, the excesses of individuals are avoided by the judgment of a group, and often by the group that will need the development. Development may be slower in the cooperative model, but it will be sounder, and it will still take place. When we are less consumed by greed and competition, as we will be with a cooperative income, we may have time and the inclination as a civilization to produce something as awesome as did our forebears.

We are not so naïve as to assume we will have (or have to have) a cooperative economy in order to accomplish development, or for that matter, income redistribution.

Will development still take place?

So we have to ask if development will still take place with the income incentives that will remain after redistribution. This cannot be predicted with certainty. It is likely, however, that development, which requires a certain type of vision, skill, and ability, is determined more by genes and experience than it is by money reward. "Developers" have to do their thing, just like many of the rest of us.

It is part of their personal satisfaction in life to accomplish this work. And as long as they are paid well, especially in relation to the salaries of others of similar skills, we can be confident that they will be happy to work.

If this conclusion is wrong, and if there were a great slowing down of development and an exodus of developers from the field, there would be both benefits and alternatives. We can benefit from slower development. Speculative development (which most of it is) often outruns demand, buildings and shopping centers remain empty, and developments contribute to the waste of capital known as bankruptcy.

Developers that manipulate politics

We can do without developers manipulating the political process to line their own pockets. They wring concessions and even grants from communities that are forced to compete with other communities for what may be uneconomic projects. If there are fewer developers, there will be less political favoritism.

As a last, and by no means least resort, communities can work on their own development by joint efforts in planning and then hiring developers and contractors to carry out their plans. The plans will be slower in accomplishment, and often better for the community input, which is now largely restricted to zoning and policing the plans of privateers, in order to protect the public health and safety.

All in all, we will probably benefit from income redistribution in the area of community and public development, whereas the activities of private companies will be little lessened or hindered by it.

Will we still have invention?

One of the most beautiful aspects of our way of doing business is creative minds that are free to produce new things. This is part of our freedom in America, and we do not want to discourage our inventors, composers, and artists by impinging on their rewards. We may even wish to encourage them.

The old saw says, "Necessity is the mother of invention." Perhaps for the pioneer, alone on the prairie, but not today, when the necessities of most of us are well provided for in the market. More important in our present civilization are the desire for leisure, curiosity, play, the drive to immortality, service, and of course, the idea of making our fortune.

Probably least considered and most important is the ability to support oneself while thinking and being creative. A fair income will support us in this process. Whether it is adequate or not remains to be seen, but very little is required for the person who is committed to creation.

Most inventors will subsist on unearned income plus a modicum of loyalty, if any, and some who are more relaxed about income or hold little or no possessory interest in their ideas will patent and copyright, to be sure that other individuals will not seize and profit from them, but then deliver any royalty income to the public via the national dividend.

So how important is the idea of making a fortune? Less, I suspect, than the opportunity to continue to invent.

The divine right of creation

Creators are driven to do their thing. And the corporation is the institution that supports most of them in this endeavor—with good salaries. Then the corporation takes their output and converts it into profit, which the corporation will continue to do with a fair income. If most of the profit goes into the national dividend, the corporation could care less. (See Chapter Three.)

We can improve the comfort and the productivity of the individual inventor by allowing that creator to subsist on the guaranteed annual income and to participate to the same extent as corporate inventors do in salary derived from their successful patents. Thus, if patents or copyrights produced a maximum quarter million dollars per year gross, or $79,000 per year net (ten times minimum wage) for any creator, that individual would retain up to that amount as salary plus the unearned income everyone gets.

Returns above these amounts would, of course, go into the national dividend to be shared with everyone. This security and incentive would probably release more creativity and invention than this country has ever seen.

Our aim is security

We are aiming at a distribution in which there will be income security for all, from the beginning of life to its end. A preliminary look at the income we all produce indicates that this is now entirely possible, such is the productivity of our technology.

Such a context of security against life's dangers and accidents will give us an entirely new outlook on our need for greed. Old age will be provided for. Education for our children will be provided for. Health needs will be provided for.

In a word, we will have *enough* money to get along on no matter what happens to us. We will no longer be beset by anxiety for the future of ourselves or our children. The present cliché that we are only three paychecks away from homelessness will not apply. In the realization of this happy state, we will find it less important to pile up riches against our worries. We will find it less necessary to give and receive large inheritances. We will tend to agree that the tremendous salaries and perquisites we now give to top management and athletes and rock stars are unnecessary as well as unfair. We may even become less possessive and more generous to those around the world who are "less developed."

We calculate the unearned income from labor

National income figures for labor income are much more accurate than those for profit, interest, and rent, for reasons that need not detain us.

Sixty percent of wages and salaries in 1990[4] amounted to about $2,200 billion. This is the amount we have suggested that is unearned in current wages and salaries, and therefore subject to

4. Internal Revenue Service, *Statistics of Income,* Spring 1992, Table B, p. 12.

transfer, with the amount up to the equal share to be kept by income receivers as they get it.

In addition, we have suggested imposition of a cap on salaries of executives and contractors that would leave them with take-home pay of no more than ten times the income of the lowest paid in the economy. The minimum wage is presently $4.25, and it will probably be adjusted to $5 or more per hour when a fair income is installed. The amount estimated for transfer under this cap on income is $300 billion.

Twenty-five hundred billion dollars divided by the 1990 population of 248 million yields a transfer estimate of capital returns in labor income of a little more than $10,000 per person per year.

Summary

Wages and salaries are now probably 90 percent comprised of returns to capital, without which we few survivors of such a holocaust (no capital) would be in a digging stick economy. Failure to recognize this fact has chained us to the nineteenth century battle between labor and management, a losing fight for labor as we pursue information technology and automated production. Honesty and prudence will require that workers (and all of us) receive our fair share of the return from capital.

In order not to upset existing practice in payment of wages and salaries, it is suggested that we transfer at least 60 percent of earned income to capital accounts and continue to tax all income in the amount needed to run the government. Labor will be better off with a fair system. Additionally, the future will be assured as automation and plant movement are unhindered, to the benefit of all owners (now everyone) and with increases in the national dividend.

The capital return from 60 percent of labor income plus a cap on salary and contract income of ten times the wage of the lowest-paid people in the economy will yield a little more than $10,000 per year of unearned income for each citizen of the U.S.A.

Chapter 5.
Smaller items and a sum

Available statistics on unearned income are either lacking or distorted. This is not surprising, since redistribution has not been the purpose of gathering the statistics, and present laws allow escape from tax of large portions of our incomes. We have estimated the amount subject to transfer from rent and royalty at $1,800 billion in 1990. From profit and interest at $2,150 billion. From wage and salary caps at $2,500 billion. This is a total subject to transfer of $6,450 billion. There is more.

Estates, gifts, and inheritance

Estate taxes of only $8 billion show up in the federal income budget. This low estate tax is explained by the fact that most estates pay no tax at all. Almost all rich people (and some of the rest of us) use living trusts rather than wills to pass on property at death.

Living trusts eliminate probate, reduce lawyers' fees, and make certain the maximum exemption is obtained. This is a neat device, for which Congress has thoughtfully provided law, which allows "step-up" in value from original to market price, and sends most estates on to heirs with no estate tax, no inheritance tax, no capital gains tax, and no publicity.

Step-up means that a property that may have cost the buyer

$50,000 can be revalued at death to its market value, which may be a million dollars, with no tax on the capital gain or to the estate. No publicity means that the most dedicated nose for news can't even find out the size of the estate.

The taxes we have proposed will not keep people from accumulating estates in order to fulfill the usual functions of savings, although they may lower the amounts. But there will be no exemptions on gifts and estates, and all inheritance or gifts from the estate of another person will constitute taxable unearned income to the recipient.

Robert Avery of Cornell University has estimated that $8 trillion will be passed on in estates in the next twenty years.[1] This is $400 billion per year. We will accept Avery's estimate. This brings our total estimate of unearned income subject to transfer to $6,850 billion.

A large total

This is more than the national income, because official figures leave out much of rent, consider all labor income as earned, and ignore inheritance altogether. Only a third of this, roughly $2,500 billion, will actually be transferred, because we will keep most of our transfer income as we get it. Only the surplus beyond the $30,000 maximum will be moved.

The Internal Revenue Service will move it

This will double the work of the IRS. They can handle it. We will keep them honest by audit. Transfers into the Fund will be quarterly. Transfers out of the Fund will be monthly.

Life insurance, pensions, annuities

Life insurance (more appropriately, "death insurance") will

1. Reported in the *Boston Globe* by Thomas Watterson. Reprinted in the *Santa Rosa Press Democrat* Oct. 13, 1991, p. E-1.

become unnecessary and will probably disappear. Its benefits are unearned income. As such, they will be taxed 100 percent. Pensions and annuities, including Social Security, unemployment insurance, disability insurance (when we get health insurance), veterans' pensions, railroad pensions, other private and government pensions will be treated similarly. They will either be renegotiated or disappear.

None of these arrangements or renegotiations will hurt individuals, or will greatly affect the income of the Fund. They will all reduce taxes and payments for these plans. Our estimate of $400 billion more income from estates and reduction of these existing transfers is very conservative.

Other sources

Crime will continue to be unreported, and restitution will continue minuscule. Our $45 billion crime bill may be reduced; this won't add to the Fund. A fair income will probably reduce embezzlement, robbery, assault, and other risky crimes a great deal, when $30,000 becomes available without risk. We may be able to leave our doors unlocked.

The underground economy

This is a weightier matter. It is variously estimated at $6 billion to over $100 billion. It consists of barter and other unreported activities. Some of it is criminal, like the drug trade, and the marijuana "industry," that brings Mendocino County, California, more income (it is said) than lumbering. Some of it is legitimate, like owner-built housing and community barn-raising. A fair income won't reduce this kind of activity, it may increase it.

We will be better off with more leisure, doing what we want to do. Even though the underground economy will contribute little money income to the Fund.

Refining the estimates

A population of 248 million in the U.S.A. in 1990 means that $6,850 billion would actually be $27,621 per person—in the absence of children. But children make a difference. They won't get as much as adults.

Children enter the equation

Any amount we allow for children will be a population policy. We all know that children cost money. And that at least for a time they cost less than adults to feed, clothe, house, and entertain. Education is a different matter, and already in the tax base.

If we were to pay an equal share for children, so that there would be no net cost to parents of having children—in fact, they would gain by having more children—that would be a population policy extremely destructive to the environment. If we paid nothing to parents for children, that would constitute a disincentive to the having of children. Parents would be poorer by each child they created. What should be our population policy?

We know that the earth is staggering under the population pressure exerted especially by ours, the consumptive society. Under these conditions we propose a population policy that will be influenced, but not coerced, by financial considerations. We propose that the first child of any mother be given half of the equal share up to the age of eighteen; that her second child be given half of that; and that no further children get any part of the unearned income that is shared.

We would thereby encourage one- and two-child families, insofar as money has an influence on this decision, and discourage larger families. Note that $82,500 per family of four or more per year is sufficient for them to rear any number of children without grave sacrifice. And that affluence, which this amount of unearned income per family means, seems to entail fewer children all by itself.

Calculations including children

According to Current Population Reports, there were 34,554,000 first children in families in the U.S.A. in 1990, 19,963,000 second children, and 10,663,000 additional children.[2] Put these numbers into the equation, and adults would get $33,783 per year, first children $16,892, and second children would be eligible for $8,446. A family of four or more would receive $92,904.

These figures are misleading by their look of accuracy. We have rounded them off to $30,000 for adults, $15,000, and $7,500 for children one and two, and $82,500 for families of two adults and any number of children. This is because we estimate conservatively, because $30,000 is perhaps enough, and because we can use the extra cash to curb inflation and save the environment. (See later chapters.)

This maximum is not net, of course. Personal income taxes at an average rate of 16 percent federal and 4 percent state and local, will reduce the maximum to a total of $66,000, still a respectable figure for family income in the 1990s.

The federal budget and earned income

When this program goes national, the federal budget will be reduced by the amounts we now spend on Social Security, farm and transportation and trade subsidies, and military subsidies and pensions (we can have rational defense instead of pork.) And we can increase spending for health, education, and infrastructure. The balance may well reduce federal expenditures by half, or $500 billion. This is another chunk we can use to combat inflation and environmental degradation.

If we add earned income up to $79,000 per year per adult to these figures on unearned income, it appears that everyone with

2. U.S. Bureau of the Census, Series P-60, Nos. 162 & 174, Tables 20.

total income under $300,000 would be better off with a fair income than they now are. This is not, as the rich would have us believe, sharing the poverty, but sharing the wealth.

Summary

When we add the unearned incomes that will be kept and transferred from profit, interest, wages and salaries, royalties, and rent, and include estimates for inheritance, without forecasting sumptuary taxes on resources like oil, we come to a total of $6,850 billion. This amounts to an average of $27,600 per citizen per year.

We do not, however, wish to encourage population growth by paying for children an amount equal to that for adults. When we reduce the amount for first children to half of that for adults, for second children to half again of that, and for third and additional children to zero, the amount per adult climbs to $33,783 per year from unearned income alone, and for the standard family of four to $92,904.

We will be satisfied with $30,000 per year per adult, and family unearned income of $82,500. This will be reduced to $66,000 by taxes. Allowed earned income increases this as much as $79,000 per year, less an average 20 percent tax. We share our affluence.

Chapter 6.
Elimination of boom and bust

I hear you complaining again: "If every adult gets $30,000 per year, wouldn't we have a boom that would choke the market with money and reduce the value of the dollar to zero? Poor people don't know how to use money. They will go crazy with spending when they get this unearned cash. What is the use of eliminating poverty with thousands of millions of paper dollars that are worthless?"

Some of your fears may be realized, briefly

The poor will tend to spend when they get money. Just like the rest of us. As you fear, they may go wild and spend it all. For awhile. When they recover from that binge, they will act like the middle class. They will spend some, work some, play some, and provide a dependable source of support for the economy.

But they won't give us worthless money

It is true that inflation is a terrible curse. I remember German postage stamps overprinted with millions of Deutschmarks. People running from paycheck to grocery store to get a few things to eat before their money became worthless. You do not exaggerate this evil. But the poor can't give it to us. Redistribution will give us the tool whereby we can restore the old saying: "Sound as a dollar."

Our present control is inadequate

Our so-called control of inflation in a "free market economy" is the Federal Reserve Board. This watchdog operates on the prime rate of interest—the rate it charges the banks for the money it lends them. The prime rate is mostly a signal. It is crude, clumsy, costly, indirect, inefficient, and discriminatory. When the "Fed" raises the prime by a quarter percent, that is supposed to cut off a boom at the pockets.

Maybe it does, maybe it doesn't

The banks are supposed to interpret this signal and raise the interest on loans to customers. Sometimes they do, sometimes they don't. Customers are supposed to respond by paying off loans, not borrowing more. Sometimes they do, sometimes they think this signals a further rise and they borrow more and buy more.

The Prime does not drive production

Interest is a small part of the cost of production. There are many more important factors that drive manufacturers and home buyers and automobile dealers to do what they do. As an officer of Friends Association of Services for the Elderly, I borrowed $2,000,000 from the bank at 13.25 percent in 1983 so we could build Friends House. The interest rate is a crude and ineffective tool in the fight against inflation.

It has to be painful

Only when the cost of credit becomes so high that a lot of economic activity is ground to a halt, the housing market stalls, plants close, automobiles and TVs fail to sell, and millions of people are thrown out of work—only then does the interest rate crush inflation. The cost is huge. The result is boom and bust. Sometimes inflation gets out of control completely. Panic buying induces more panic buying, and losses become astronomical as prices go out of sight. Which is the same thing as saying the money becomes worthless. This is the danger we live with. Boom and bust is what we have. (As I write, the Fed is doing better with its balancing act. The interest rate is still ineffective against hyper-inflation.)

Income redistribution would not drive us to inflation

Even if the poor get more money, they are a small part of the economy. Their temporary increased spending will be easily offset by a small reduction for the rest of us. That reduction is already allowed for by setting the initial distribution of unearned income at $30,000, instead of the $33,000+ calculated in Chapter 5.

The spending of 250 million people adds up very quickly with a small amount for each. If the stipend of each of us were reduced by thirty-five cents per month, this would reduce total spending by a billion dollars per year. Thirty-five dollars per month reduction per person would result in a total spending reduction of $100 billion per year.

Who would notice $35 out of a monthly unearned income of almost $3,000? Reduction of a billion dollars spending would be noticed in the economy. Reduction of $100 billion would be the two-by-four that got the donkey's attention. Inflation would be curbed. Positively. Absolutely. Without question. And it would cost us practically nothing.

How income redistribution works on inflation

We have suggested that $2,500 billion will be transferred with income redistribution from those who have too much to those who have too little. The transfer will require time and a place, the Fund, for operation. No matter how quick the turnaround, this Fund will approach two trillion dollars as a working balance. The balance gives us an unparalleled opportunity to control inflation, to the point where there will be none.

The Internal Revenue Service will be our agent

The collector and disburser of the Fund—probably the Internal Revenue Service, which already does this work—will be given the following instruction by the Congress: "Add to or subtract from the Fund amounts necessary to maintain the integrity of the dollar." The rest requires watching price indexes and arithmetic.

If inflation threatens by a tenth of one percent, the IRS will simply subtract from its payout to us an amount sufficient to bring it down to "normal." That money will be withheld and go into the bank. It may later be used to boost our spending if deflation threatens. The single criterion of a sound dollar is all we have to mandate by law. The rest is bookkeeping.

The lag between collection and payment is valuable

Caution in the big change will prevent us from making the error of allowing inflation *or* depression. We will build in a lag, probably three months, between the time we collect the taxes and pay out the national dividend. This will do the trick.

Any spending fuels inflation. If you haul money out of the bank in order to buy an automobile or take a global tour, that adds to inflationary pressure. If you borrow money that you and the bank create for those purposes, and you buy inventory or a plant or a house, that fuels inflation. If you buy stocks on margin, that drives up the prices on the market. If you throw wild parties or buy up art at auction or play polo, that puts money into the income stream and results in a multiplied effect on spending.

Deflation is the other side of the coin

On the other hand, if you pay your mortgage ahead of time, that takes money out of the income stream, and results in deflation. If you save more, and the banks can't find profitable investments for what you put away, the money sits there idle, out of the income stream, and reduces demand. No money spent equals deflation. If you are unemployed and have only welfare dollars to spend, which are a fourth of the amount you were making while employed, that means deflation.

Money that is already there

When we redistribute income that is already in the stream of demand, that doesn't take it out of business. It is still there, doing its job of running the economy. Spending will be heavier on the necessities of life as formerly poor people increase their demands for food and housing and clothes and automobiles and televisions, while it will be lighter on the extras.

The system will respond

The American system is nothing if not flexible, responding to changes in demand even before they become evident to most of us. The lag between income to the Fund and outgo from it will give us the leeway to make the adjustments in spending that will be needed to keep the dollar sound. And that lag will also give industry time to readjust to changes in the product mix. Our agents, the IRS, have to watch it carefully, and adjust accordingly—a bookkeeper's job.

Unemployment and our environmental impact

We have concentrated on inflation. We have not forgotten deflation. Unemployment will be a thing of the past. In this setting we can seriously discuss the impact of our industrial system on the environment. We shall devote a later chapter to this subject. We can deflate our spending and thereby our destruction of the environment by instructing the bookkeepers to take money out of the fund before they send us our checks.

Elimination of boom and bust

This will not result in unemployment in our labor-short economy. With a sustained, certain income, we can all become whistleblowers on polluters and the breakers of environmental law. We will no longer have loggers teaming up with lumber companies to eliminate the spotted owl as they clear-cut our old-growth forests. We can save species without economic reprisal.

The national debt can be good for you
If we worry about the effect on the economy of building a surplus in the Fund, aside from employees' temptation to pilfer it, which we will consider in the chapter on administration, we should bethink ourselves of the national debt.

Here we have a huge ball and chain around our necks and the necks of our children, which we have heretofore seen as a mechanism of extracting money from the poor to pay the rich. (The rich deny this, of course, but the only way we can all suffer is through inflation.)

The ball and chain will be off our necks
When we have income redistribution, the ball and chain will be removed. The interest paid by all of us will be received by all of us. We may even be able in future to discern the advantage of the debt in its ability to soak up surpluses from the Fund as we wind down the economy to sustainability. Pay off the debt with those surpluses. This will stabilize the boom. And don't forget, with income redistribution we will never have a bust.

Summary
Control of inflation in the present economy is poorly done by manipulation of the interest rate, a tool which is crude, indirect, inefficient, and discriminatory. The interest rate sends a mixed signal and only when it becomes coercive will it trigger a bust, which is an extremely expensive way to curb inflation.

93

Income redistribution, on the other hand, will give us a tool whereby to fight inflation directly. In the interval between receipt of unearned income and paying it out on an equal basis, we can subtract an amount sufficient to reduce the supply of money in spenders' hands, or add an amount to increase it if deflation threatens, and thus make the dollar as sound as we used to think it was when it was tied to gold.

Unemployment will never threaten when every citizen has a guaranteed income of $30,000 every year. And the national debt will be a boon in fighting the boom-bust cycle.

Chapter 7.
Welfare, subsidy, and dignity

We have so far seen that a fair income will eliminate unemployment, allow us to control inflation, reduce crime, and allow everyone previously unheard-of freedom to determine their lives and achieve their potential.

Now let us concentrate on its most direct achievement: the elimination of poverty; and simultaneously with that, the demise of the welfare system. These are the aims of other writers on the guaranteed annual income, but they are aims mostly unrealized, even in their rosiest projections.

President Nixon's impassioned plea

On December 13, 1970, Richard Nixon spoke to the decennial White House Conference on Children. He had thrown out the speeches and notes of his writers, and at dawn that morning began to write his own words:

> On August 11, 1969, I proposed that for the first time in America's history we establish a floor under the income of every American family with children. We called it the Family Assistance Plan. It has in turn been called the most important piece of social legislation in our nation's history. You know the story of this legislation. In

April it passed the House of Representatives by a margin of almost two to one. Then it became mired down in the Senate. . . .

In the last ten years alone the number of children on welfare has nearly tripled, to more than 6 million. Six million children. Six million children caught up in an unfair and tragic system that rewards people for not working instead of providing the incentives for self-support and independence, that drives families apart instead of holding them together, that brings welfare snoopers into their homes, that robs them of pride and destroys dignity. I want to change all that.

The welfare system has become a consuming, monstrous, inhuman outrage against the community, against the family, against the individual—and most of all against the very children whom it was meant to help. We have taken long strides toward ending racial segregation, but welfare segregation can be almost as insidious. . . .

I remember that my older brother had tuberculosis for five years. The hospital and doctor bills were more than we could afford. In the five years before he died, my mother never bought a new dress. We were poor by today's standards. I suppose we were poor even by Depression standards. But the wonder of it was that we did not know we were poor. Somehow my mother and father with their love, with their pride, their courage and their self-sacrifice were able to create a spirit of self-respect in our family so that we had no sense of being inferior to others who had more than we had.

Today's welfare child is not so fortunate. . . . No matter how much pride and courage his parents have, he knows they are poor—and he can feel that soul-stifling, patronizing attitude that follows the dole.

Perhaps he watches while a case-worker—himself trapped in a system that wastes, on policing, talents that could be used for helping—while this case-worker is forced by the system to poke around in the child's apartment, checking on how the money is spent or whether his mother might be hiding his father in the closet. This sort of indignity is hard enough on the mother—enough of a blow to her pride and self-respect—but think what it must mean to a sensitive child.

We have a chance now to give that child a chance—a chance to grow up without having his schoolmates throw in his face the fact that he is on welfare, and without making him feel that he is therefore something less than the other children.

Our task is not only to lift people out of poverty, but from the standpoint of the child to erase the stigma of welfare and illegitimacy and apartness—to restore pride and dignity and self-respect.[1]

Welfare has changed little

We have come a little way toward dignity since President Nixon wrote these words, having eliminated the man-in-the-house rule. One might say we have almost achieved the standard of Mexico, where conjugal visits to prisoners are allowed.

But we still have to check the welfare client's income, the whereabouts of the father, whether and how much the father is working, whether the mother is working or seeking a job or in a job training program.

1. Quoted in Moynihan, Daniel P., *The Politics of a Guaranteed Income*, New York, Random House, 1973, pp. 539-41.

We assume fraud

We assume welfare fraud and check every way we can think of that clients might be cheating. Are they eligible for Medicaid, food stamps, free school lunches? The general public knows, standing in the grocery check-out line, if food stamps are being used for luxurious items, if the welfare client they follow out the store is driving a late model car. The opprobrium is pervasive and obnoxious, just as it was when Richard Nixon spoke.

We still vote welfare, not a guaranteed income

Those of us who do not suffer the indignity of having to apply for welfare seem to find it possible to inflict this system on other human beings—perhaps with pangs of sympathy and remorse, but not enough to keep the Senate from voting down the president's plan in 1970.

We are comfortable

We can sit in our easy chairs or around the committee table and see statistics rise on urban crime, on illegitimate children, on single mothers on welfare, on drug abuse, and put the people behind these statistics into another class of human beings—people we call lazy, incompetent, shiftless, and no-good. We will see that these "others" do not starve, unless they cannot or will not meet our requirements that they beg, that is, fill out forms and be "investigated"; and now work.

The system is inhuman

It is the desire of those who run the country and make the laws that we not allow people to starve in the midst of our affluence. But this is what we say: we are afraid that welfare will "cost too much," that it will encourage indolence, that people who are as greedy as we will rip us off, will be lay-abouts who don't want to work, who will lie and cheat in order to get a handout, and will be irresponsible parents.

So we police them. We investigate them and deprive them of freedom and dignity. Social work often becomes a disgusting task instead of a helping profession. And what we do to poor people ensures that they fulfill our worst expectations of them. The system is not human, it is not the American ideal, it is not ethical, it is not compassionate, and it is counterproductive.

Congress and the guaranteed income

Why did Congress in 1969 and 1970 almost pass a guaranteed annual income that was labeled a Family Assistance Plan? Because the country was erupting in urban violence, of which the 1965 Watts riots in Los Angeles were the most terrifying example. Watts made political scientists and legislators wonder if the fabric of government was coming apart. Business leaders became sensitive. If law and order could not be maintained, the system would come down in shambles.

We have learned to be more repressive, less sensitive, to the Los Angeles riots of 1992.

The Senate flubbed

The Senate failed to adopt this plan because the worst of the violence seemed to be spent by the time they got to debating it, because they did not fully understand the plan, because they lacked the political leadership to put it through, because the National Welfare Rights Organization under George Wiley's fire-eating leadership wanted $2,400 annually per family of four instead of the paltry $1,600 bone the bill threw to the poor.

Because conservatives did not want to pay that much, because liberals wanted more, up to the poverty level of income (George McGovern, a presidential candidate at that time, argued for $6,500 per family of four), because welfare workers, whose jobs were at stake, defended their self-interest, and because the president's support of the bill was inept, too little and too late. So it failed.

What have we learned?

Twenty-odd years later, we are still suffering from this fiasco. Riots are still happening, welfare rolls are still climbing, illegitimacy is still soaring, single parent families are still increasing in numbers, crime and drugs are worse problems than ever, unemployment among blacks is still five to ten times what it is among whites, hope is absent in a large segment of our population, and despair is everywhere. We seem to have learned nothing, and to care less.

We give to the already affluent

Meanwhile, we subsidize the rich. Farm subsidies still go for the most part to the holders of large tracts of land. Subsidies to higher education are for the benefit of those who can afford to go to college. These include land grants, building funds, operating expenses from legislatures, science foundations, research allocations, military contracts, and practically every other source of funds including tuition, scholarships, and fees.

Tariffs, trade subsidies, embargoes, and trade restrictions are mostly for the gain of wealthy corporations and individuals. The income tax is skewed to subsidize the rich, as in (the usual) small capital gains tax, deductions for contributions, depreciation, real estate taxes, mortgage and other interest payments, expenses for "doing business," and so on.

The 1990 lid on taxes was 28 percent no matter how much income you received (under certain circumstances, 33 percent.) The tax is now only slightly progressive. It is, to all intents and purposes, a flat tax at a high rate to compensate for 109 loopholes.

Discrimination in taxes

These are but a few examples of a large category of tax policies that make the rich richer, the poor and the middle class poorer. One that few of us have thought of is the so-called "conscription tax," consisting of wages foregone and the costs of evasion, which are so unfairly and unequally assessed when we have conscription under Selective Service, a law that is always in the background even with a volunteer army.

Conscription settles on a few the facing of the death penalty for defending the life-style the rest of us enjoy, while paying inductees a pittance, shortening and reducing their earnings expectancy, and subjecting them to conditions we wouldn't foist upon our dog. According to authors Larry Sjaastad and Ronald Hansen, "As a tax, conscription under Selective Service is brutally inefficient—virtually in a class by itself."[2]

The right to a fair income

It is curious that with all of the attention, time, speeches, confrontations, riots, sit-ins, demonstrations, thinking by Presidential aides and Congressional assistants, a statement signed by 1,200 economists in favor of the guaranteed annual income, and the Los Angeles riots of 1992, no one seems to have thought of the idea that the poor had a right to anything. Even the Welfare Rights Organization proceeded on the same assumption as the lawmakers and the President that the poor were to be given something, small or large, that came out of the pockets of the well-to-do by taxation. Charity by extortion. Indeed, the rights they asserted were a plea for compassion and generosity in an affluent society, not the *right*

2. More detail on subsidies to the rich can be found, as can the article by Sjaastad and Hansen, in Boulding, Kenneth E. and Martin Pfaff, *Redistribution to the Rich and the Poor,* Belmont, Calif., Wadsworth Publishing Co. 1972, esp. pp. 181-204. Martin and Anita Pfaff estimate that the redistribution from the poor to the rich via taxes in 1965 was $64 billion.

to ownership. They wanted more equality of income, but lacked the rationale of unearned income that makes the case compelling.

The right to dignity

This is a demeaning spectacle in view of the facts. President Nixon spoke of restoring dignity to single parents and to children and to poor families because there would be no welfare worker breathing down their backs to see if they were cheating on the eligibility requirements under his Family Assistance Plan. But the indignity still remains if the recipient of a dole from the public purse knows that she (or he) has no right to it; it comes to her out of the compassion and goodness of heart of her betters.

There is a vast difference between a guaranteed annual income plan conceived out of the compassion of the wealthy or their fear of riots and property damage, and one that proceeds on the premise that the unearned income of the economy belongs equally to all of us.

It really means, in the latter case, that every person can hold up his or her head, that every person knows that he or she is not taking anything from anybody else that is rightfully theirs. It really means, in the latter case, that those of us who are better off will no longer be stealing the patrimony of the poor (as we do every day under present laws.)

We won't be able to feel guilt for being better off than others; to feel superior simply because others are poor. They will not be poor. The "poor" will be as wealthy as the privileged by means of their ownership in resources received from the earth and from our ancestors and common knowledge. (They will have smaller incomes if they don't work.)

Unearned income will no longer be stolen

If you are better off than someone else under a fair income, it is because you work and earn that income that belongs to you.

(John Smith and the Puritan work ethic in a better setting.) No one will be able to fault anyone for giving or taking what is not theirs; none of us will any longer be doing this. Dignity will become real. And the case for equal distribution of unearned income, contrary to received doctrine, is correct.

The costs of law and order

It has probably not escaped the attention of the governors of our country that the only avenues for income open to too many inner city black youth—drug dealing, mugging the stranger, prostitution—keep them out of the mainstream and preoccupied with these minor crimes.

These crimes don't bother the movers and shakers in our society, who don't walk in the inner city at night, or if they do, they go slumming with bodyguards. Crime in the streets and prostitution may be calculated costs of law and order to our leaders. If these minor offenses tend to get out of hand, our leaders build more prisons.

Welfare, too, is a considerable cost they (and all of us) have to pay in order to keep on doing business as usual.

Prisons are one of our greatest and most shameful growth industries. Now that three violent crimes will cost a person a lifetime of free board and room behind bars, we will engage in an orgy of prison building, which is only the beginning.

It costs $25,000 per year to give this service to each prisoner (more than a college education), and according to the reasoning of the governor of California, this will *save* us money because those prisoners will not be out on the streets to commit their fourth and fifth violent crimes.

Our leaders seem to have no ideas for *preventing* those crimes in the first place. Government will have to eliminate welfare, provide a system of income management that will give a job to everyone who is willing to work, and really deal with violence, drugs, and prostitution if it expects to maintain credibility with an electorate that can read the signs.

Poverty weighs us down

Mothers on welfare are like other mothers in most respects. They love their children and want them to grow up healthy, happy, and successful. They know all about the perils of the culture of poverty, and yet they cannot help but hope . . . can it be different? Middle class sympathizers talk about empowerment. Black leaders try for discipline and pride. But the culture of poverty is ever present, bearing down, stifling, suffocating. Peer pressure is exerted toward the only avenues there are to any kind of life, difficult and derelict though it may be.

Money will certainly make a difference, but a generation or two may have to pass before the difference transforms that environment.

Fair income in the inner city

The realization of a national fair annual income will ultimately turn it around. This proposal will revolutionize the lives of poor people in the inner city. The inadequate education available to inner city children will have to change.

Parents will insist on it. They will have time and the spirit to go to their meetings, demand proper service and attention, keep up their homes and neighborhoods, oust sick and malevolent politicians, engage in the activities that will eliminate crime and violence, hang up the drugs along with their dealers, make prostitution unnecessary, and give opportunity to every boy and girl in America.

The Pledge of Allegiance will again become an article of faith in the minds of children who are taught to say it in our schools. We may not even find a person any longer who *wants* to burn the flag.

Jails will become museums

We will probably almost empty the jails, since lack of demand will dry up the drug trade, and the large proportion of jail inmates from that source will diminish radically. When a life of opportunity and promise opens before every young person in the country regardless of circumstance or heredity, few will want to blight those prospects by engaging in petty crimes and peculations. There will be no need to steal for bread.

Without the nursery of petty crime and jail schooling, the supply of hardened criminals will diminish drastically. The jail population will never become zero in our complicated society, but it will no longer be a burgeoning growth industry.

They'll be just like us

Think of the education young people (and old) will receive in travel! College, why not? Apprentice to any vocation and get on with your life? Of course. Marry at a later age, have one or two children, and stick with your spouse? Nothing to make welfare more attractive, since welfare will be defunct, and the incentive to maintain the family lies in a fair income. Two can live more cheaply than one, and still receive the same income.

The poor will turn out to be just like the middle class, when they get money. Opportunity now knocks at their door. A fair income really goes to the heart of welfare, and the word will take on new meaning when this program goes into effect. President Nixon was right in his words, perhaps in his heart as well. Dignity is really the bottom line. And dignity will flourish as it is nourished with respect—respect for all of us in our right to the freely produced and delivered good things of the earth.

Summary

President Nixon is perhaps the best known proponent of the guaranteed annual income, which he proposed to Congress in

1969 in response to the Watts riots in 1965. The House passed his plan, but the Senate blocked it. Mr. Nixon's speech introducing his proposal sets forth the demeaning character of welfare.

$30,000 per year per citizen will take the place of welfare payments, eliminating poverty as well as the police aspects of the welfare worker's job. It will not eliminate necessary services performed by social workers who take care of mentally and physically disabled people. It will reduce subsidies to the rich, empty the jails, and make our system of income distribution fair.

Chapter 8.
An environmental impact report

Population balance

If balance between our burgeoning population and limited resources[1] were the only positive effect we could imagine, and if all other results of income redistribution were negative, it would still be imperative that we install the new program. We who live in the industrialized nations (the so-called "developed" world) tend to think that the population "problem" belongs to the Third World ("developing nations").

Third World inhabitants tend to believe that the problem belongs to us, since we have raped the world first and now try to stop them from doing the same thing. They call it ethnic murder.

Both have some of the truth

There is truth in both camps. Biologist Wayne H. Davis has calculated that because of American affluence, an American baby creates twenty-five times the impact on the environment that an Indian baby does.[2] It is also true that poor people in search of food and fuel destroy forests and fields in their attempts to survive.

1. "Anyone who believes exponential growth can go on forever in a finite world is either a madman or an economist."—Kenneth Boulding, quoted in *Fourth World Review,* No. 52, London, 1992, p. 14.
2. *The New Republic,* Jan. 10, 1970.

It is hard to overestimate the disastrous consequences of our population "bomb," as Paul Ehrlich called it in 1968. And this bomb belongs to all of us, rich or poor, wherever we live on the planet. (Paul and Anne Ehrlich's 1990 book is entitled *The Population Explosion.*)

Ehrlich: Sterilization

Paul Ehrlich suggested in 1968 a formidable program that is proportional to the seriousness of the problem. He called for chemicals in the water supply to induce mass sterilization, increased taxation on those who have more than a replacement number of children, abortion as a right of every woman, and overcoming the opposition of the Church.

On the world scene, he favored the military concept of triage, which divides casualties into those who cannot be saved, those who can, and those who will suffer but can make it on their own—with medical aid only for those who can be helped. He put India into the list of those countries that cannot be saved, and said we should offer India no food or other aid. (In 1990, with the bomb exploding and with India in worse shape than twenty-two years earlier, he and Anne did not mention triage.) Ehrlich would have sterilized all Indian males with three or more children in 1968, and he recommended tying all grants to population control.[3]

Chasteen: Compulsory birth control

Edgar Chasteen states that a policy of compulsory birth control is our number-one national priority. He recommends a two-per-family limit on children, and says that an ideal contraceptive is an absolute necessity.

3. Ehrlich, Paul R., *The Population Bomb,* N. Y., Ballantine Books, 1968. Paul and Anne Ehrlich, *The Population Explosion* N. Y., Simon and Schuster, 1990.

Meanwhile, he advocates the contraception we have, including vasectomies, tubal ligations, and abortions. He says that recipients of our foreign aid must do as we should do, and calls for education in implementation of his plans.[4]

Lorenz: Eighth deadly sin

Konrad Lorenz calls overpopulation one of our "eight deadly sins." He says that "Humanity threatens to do what living systems almost never do, namely to suffocate in itself." Worst of all in this apocalypse, the highest and noblest properties and faculties of "man," the ones rightly valued as specifically human, are apparently the first to perish.

"We who live in densely populated civilized countries, especially in large cities, no longer realize how much we are in want of warm-hearted human affection." But his cure for all ills is exposure of the dangers, the task to which he sets himself in the book.[5] We are supposed to be intelligent.

Sell your birth rights—Boulding

Kenneth Boulding, in his book, *The Meaning of the Twentieth Century,* states the problem in his chapter titled "The Great Transition" and his solution in the one titled "The Population Trap." First, the problem:

> One of the first impacts of postcivilized medicine and medical knowledge on civilized society is a large and immediate reduction in the death rate, especially in infant mortality.
> This is seldom if ever accompanied by a similar

4. Chasteen, Edgar R., *The Case for Compulsory Birth Control,* Englewood Cliffs, Prentice-Hall. 1971.
5. Lorenz, Konrad, *Civilized Man's Eight Deadly Sins,* N. Y., Harcourt Brace, Jovanovich, 1973.

decrease in birth rate, and hence the first impact of post-civilized techniques on a previously stable civilized society is a tremendous upsurge in the rate of population increase. This increase may be so large that the society is incapable of adapting itself to it, and incapable in particular of devoting sufficient resources to the education of its unusually large cohorts of young people.

We therefore have the tragic situation that the alleviation of much human misery and suffering in the short run may result in enormous insoluble problems in a longer period."[6]

His solution is to issue certificates at birth allowing each woman to have two children during her lifetime, and to allow a market to develop in these certificates.

Provide economic penalties—Brown

Lester Brown told us in 1974 that we *have* to limit world population to fewer than 6 billion people. That looked more possible fifteen years ago than in 1989, when we passed speedily through 5 billion without a pause for reflection.

His recipe for alleviation of the people problem is family planning, changing social conditions among which he includes an adequate, assured food supply for everyone, and equal rights for women. He would also eliminate U.S. income tax deductions for an unlimited number of children, eliminate French child care allowances, eliminate subsidized maternity leaves, limit government subsidized housing and scholarships to families with two or fewer children, and give special bonuses to single people. Under

6. Boulding, Kenneth E., *The Meaning of the Twentieth Century*, New York, Harper and Row, 1964, p. 25.

his proposals social security payments would also be linked to family planning.[7]

Note that Brown includes several economic deprivations for excessive child production, but no incentives for family limitation. Every punishment can be flipped into an incentive, but offering to take away what we have is a hard way to secure votes.

No powerful tools yet

None of these experts comes up with a solution to the population problem that matches their analysis or their sometimes draconian remedies. Poisoning the water is not a very acceptable remedy. Compulsory sterilization docs not sell well. Boulding himself thought his license and marketing idea a bit silly.

Tea parties and self education have not touched the centers of power, and will not in future, any more than in the past, keep us from drowning in our own pollution. The experts have not so far conceived of a powerful tool which is at the same time attractive and effective.

$30,000 per year is a powerful tool

Income redistribution is such a tool. Experience everywhere shows a high positive correlation between income and a personal, self-imposed limit on the number of children per family. Western European countries are, in fact, subsidizing children in an effort to stem their declining populations.

There is every reason to believe that when income is sufficient, and particularly when security of income becomes a reality, people will self-regulate their children to a number that will balance with resources. And that the balance can be modified by changing the income support for children.

People may think they need children to care for them in their

7. Brown, Lester R. *In the Human Interest,* New York, W.W. Norton, 1974.

old age. This is less true in America than in India, where children don't think of abandoning their parents, and where welfare and social security are foreign concepts. But an adequate income guaranteed to everyone for life will remove this perceived need, whether or not children support the elderly. Thus one of the biggest arguments for more children will be removed wherever a fair income is enacted.

Unearned income will provide the incentive

We are about to see emerge in the democratic, affluent West the perfectly fair and practical and pleasant proposition that we redistribute unearned income, which will provide the proper incentive for family limitation. A first child benefit limited to half that for an adult and a second child benefit of one-fourth the adult's will make it easy for any couple to rear two children. No further benefits for children will not keep anyone from having more children, if they want to earn the money to support them. But everyone will know what that costs, and prudence will once again make us as provident as Indian tribes always have been, or as the Irish turned out to be after the famine of 1841.

The Irish famine of 1841

Caroline Bird and Kenneth Boulding both present the case of the Irish after the potato famine, when half the population of eight million perished by starvation. According to Bird, the Irish responded in two constructive ways, by limiting procreation and by emigration.

"The first thing they did was to turn their heads around on having babies. In the absence of contraceptive devices of any kind, or even any rationale for birth control, the Irish cut their birth rate from one of the highest in the world to one of the lowest. The result is that Ireland has fewer people in 1971 than it had 130 years earlier.

"Heaven only knows how they do it, but the rumor is that they are good Catholics and simply abstain from the kind of sex that results in pregnancy."[8]

How they do it

Boulding claims to know how they do it: "The population of Ireland has increased very little in over a hundred years, partly as a result of increased emigration, but more as a result of limitation of births.

"In this case the limitation was achieved through late marriages and the imposition of a strongly Puritan ethic upon the young people which seems to have the effect of strongly limiting the number of children born out of wedlock. It is striking that one of the most successful examples of population control should have taken place in a Roman Catholic country, one, moreover, in which Catholicism takes an unusually puritanical form."[9]

We can limit population easily

We need not make moral judgments about the way people react to incentives to have more or fewer children, nor imply that all such decisions rest at bottom on economic considerations; they don't. We do need to realize that people are smart enough to know the economic consequences of having more children, and they probably react rationally to this knowledge.

We turn to the Commission on Population Growth and the American Future, which in 1971 figured that it cost $150,000 to bring up two children and send them through college if you count the money the mother could have earned if she had worked at a job instead of staying home to rear them. (This figures the woman's pay at $324 per month, $1.94 per hour, a conservative wage.)

8. Bird, Caroline, *The Crowding Syndrome,* New York. David McKay Co., 1972, p. 275.
9. Op. Cit., p. 130.

If we adjust this amount with the Consumer Price Index, the same package would have cost that couple $481,000 in 1989. If we adjust that amount for eighteen years into the future with an average inflation rate of 3 percent, the same package would cost that couple $795,000.

Such are the wonders of inflation. Of course we will expect to get inflation under control long before the passage of eighteen years. Do couples consider economics when planning children? They do if they have any money.

"America First" in population balance

Why do Western peoples have to lead the way? Because we are the people of the world most destructive of the environment. Some say that it is only Americans who give the world the population problem, ignoring both human and planetary devastation wrought by poor people in the tropics as they struggle to survive.

We shall be Americans First in this area, and we will, through our position in history and our democratic institutions, lead the world in a program that will bring population down to manageable limits everywhere.

People will make their own decisions

Family planning from above is not notably successful in limiting population. The motivation must be there before the method, and people have limited population growth without the most modern devices. Primitive tribes have managed to fit their numbers to their food supplies without the over-production of babies who were later to starve.

The Irish have cut their population way down despite the strictures of the Church. The Oneida Community under the direction of John Humphrey Noyes made the decision and did not produce a single baby in a population of more than two hundred from 1848 to 1868. Motivation is the key, which an assured monthly income for life will be. And the means, which are available, can be advertised and provided.

We will eliminate much human misery and environmental degradation by simple income redistribution.

We will consume less

Thus the first great environmental effect of income redistribution is that there will be fewer of us in twenty years, not more, to wreak our havoc on the good earth, our home. The second is that we will consume less.

The emphasis throughout this discussion has been on saving: what you will do with your surplus; the security that a guaranteed income will give everyone, and how we can all insure this by putting aside a half million dollar estate. This means frugality, not over-consumption.

In addition to this Puritan-ingrained outlook, which a great many of us share, we will have an easy time and a fair process for reducing our national consumption. "Buy-less" campaigns, and higher quality, longer lasting appliances and cars will become slogans.

Advertising for more junk will be reduced as the opportunities to make millions in national and international markets is obliterated. Consumer efforts to reduce our profligacy will be mounted. And the national consensus to reduce our requirements at the Fund level will be seriously debated and decided every year.

The damage to the environment will be reduced and some of it restored as we consciously lower our intake of energy and consumption goods while improving our quality of life.

Who is "taking" whom?

The word that is all the rage among our most greedy people as I write this is "taking." If all of us reduce the value of a piece of private property a small percentage by passing an environmental law, we are supposed to repay that private owner the amount of the "damage." This practically nullifies environmental law.

Besides its questionable moral ground (Who "took" all of the property in the first place? And who now "takes" its value every day from the rest of us in rent?), this word will have no standing under income redistribution. If the value goes down, the owner will have less rent to pay. And the rent, as unearned income, will all be "taken" for redistribution, anyway. No one will get rich by being paid by the rest of us for a value reduction.

The green pastures of agriculture

A fair income will lead us into greener pastures. It will save the agricultural lands of this country from wind and water erosion, save the remaining old growth forests from destruction, plant new trees, renew our cities into more habitable places for children and adults, provide the means by which people can easily establish and maintain new cooperative communities, and see that laws are strictly enforced against polluters.

A fair income will solve the farm problem

We know that large farms, often corporately owned and controlled, with monoculture and commercial fertilizer and pesticides and soil mining and ground water pollution and erosive practices, are taking over much of the farming landscape in the richest agricultural resource in the world, the U.S.A.

We know that where these lands lie next to cities, sprawling development, single family homes, smog, and monotonous replications of fast food outlets and automobile retailers and shopping centers are paving over the fertility and productivity and destroying the clean air of the farms now being sold for temporary dollars and a polluted environment.

We know that small farms and small communities produce healthy, independent citizens and stable, caring institutions all of which wither and die when the corporate farming of large acreage takes over in the land. We have no effective means of reversing these trends under the current economic dispensation.

Large farms, small farms, development

Fund income will affect the farm problem in several important ways. When government farm subsidies are replaced by transfers among people, the anomaly of $50,000-$100,000 payments to single or corporate owners of large tracts will disappear.

When rents and profits are placed in the Fund and speculative land holding for capital gains is no longer a driving force for land acquisition, the price of land will drop to the point where it reflects productivity and position rather than gambling.

There are plenty of people ready and willing to acquire and work small farms. What stops them today is lack of funds to buy land in competition with the big operators and inability to compete with the buyers of big machinery.

Farmers will personally subsidize

Where small farmers are a competitive sector in a world of monopoly capitalists, they will probably still have to subsidize their own farming activity, as they have done heretofore by long hours and other jobs. But Fund income will supply them the wherewithal to operate. Lower land prices will give them the opportunity to buy land. They will be able to compete where subsidies no longer go to the holders of large tracts as a reward for land being kept out of production.

And small farmers take care of their land. They have a history of crop rotation, planting trees and hedgerows, water and land conservation, and leaving land to the next generation in better shape than they found it. Organic farming, with composting, no pesticides or chemicals, and healthy food for the market, is the province of the small farmer. A straight line of reasoning leads from $30,000 per year to saving agriculture.

Cities will be concentrated

Fund income will also have a strong counter-effect on urban sprawl and suburbanization, since the profit factor will be taken out of the urge to sell developers the land next to cities. Stubborn farmers can even now be found who refuse the enticement of the quick dollar in selling out their inherited or long and lovingly cared-for establishments.

When the profit is eliminated from the sale of land and passed on to the rest of us through the Fund, few farmers will be tempted. They will also find it highly desirable to continue farming close to the cities with their supplementary Fund incomes and the market that location provides.

Fund income will change our cities

The effects of Fund income will therefore be considerable on city sprawl as well as on the farm problem. As it costs more to run an automobile, and as architects and planners turn their attention to more rewarding life styles, cities will also become communities. It will be possible to develop cooperative housing in cities despite bad street configuration and the present high costs of existing houses.

Architecture will accommodate more and more the needs of people rather than the automobile. Gardens will proliferate, and convenient modes of transportation will be built both with the money from $30,000 per year and with the hands and skills of inhabitants.[10]

Housing costs will drop

The Fund will also have a positive effect on lowering inner city housing costs. Speculative price rise will be squeezed out of

---

10. Forerunners of these ideas will be found in the delightful book, *A Pattern Language,* by Christopher Alexander, et al., op. cit.

these transactions, and land costs will drop to reflect only position desirability. Construction costs will no longer be distorted by building for the rich. The ability to take time off to build your own house will be possible with a built-in transfer income that never stops.

The wage scales for the building crafts may come down a bit with this educated unskilled labor available, but carpenters and plumbers and electricians need not worry. Their high skill abilities will be in great demand in many other jobs in our changing economy.

Cooperative housing

The intentional community is another matter entirely. The yearning for living closely with neighbors you know and respect is a constantly recurring theme in American history. We know what it's like to be lonely here, and we've seen ourselves as alienated individuals reflected in David Riesman's *The Lonely Crowd.*

Practically every community that has ever been started has been a protest against this feeling of alienation and loneliness as well as a design for a better life—one in which competition is replaced by help, estrangement by friendliness and love, put-down and exploitation by equality and justice.

And hundreds of them have succeeded over time. There are thousands in existence right now in this land of free competition and the rat race.

The economic environment is now hostile to community

The main trouble for community right now is that the legal, social, and economic environment for cooperative housing is distinctly hostile in America. Land cost is prohibitive, loans are not available for co-ops, urban places are already built and inhospitable for cooperative occupancy, and the government is unfriendly.

With income redistribution, some of these conditions will

change considerably. The desire will remain strong, as it has for centuries. Land costs will drop as the profit from renting becomes part of the general Fund. People will be able to commit their time and talents to building their own houses if they want to take time off from work. And in cooperative groups this is much facilitated by the availability of the necessary skills.

Most importantly, people will have the money they need to build cooperative communities. Banks may not see the cooperative economy in a different light than is now the case, but that is likely. And cooperative banks need only follow the example of the Caja Laboral. The outlook for community is better in the future than it has been in the past. With income redistribution, this organization for human betterment will grow everywhere in the land.

More care for the environment

The positive effects of this income change are very large: the banishment of the loss-of-job worry and the political power that that single factor will liberate, and what I shall call the conscience effect. The negative effect is small: that the present underclass will have more money with which to consume.

We have already dealt with this in the chapter on Boom and Bust. When people no longer fear that their income will dry up if they lose their jobs, but know instead that they will have enough to live on during any emergency or transition period without any qualifying restrictions, the feeling of independence, security, and freedom this will give them is enormous and liberating.

They will no longer clamor for military facilities and bases and waste dumps and airplane factories in their back yards because these things give jobs. They will no longer be blinded to the environmental effects of acid rain and smoke stack disease and carcinogenic substances because they feel we must produce these things in order not to lose jobs to the competition.

Companies will no longer be able to depend on the political

support of lumberjacks and loggers and mill workers to cut down our magnificent old growth forests because these workers will not fear losing their only means of livelihood. We will be able as a nation to look at the environmental effects of our corporate greed without the bias engendered by the cry, "Jobs will be lost."

"Pork barrel" politics will have a hard time in Congress. Leaders may be thrown out by constituents who really have a concern for the future of the planet, and we know by present surveys that these include at least 75 percent of us.

Whistle-blowers will blow

The conscience effect has to do with whistle blowers, some of the bravest and most environmentally conscious among us who even today are willing to risk persecution and job loss in order to make companies live up to the environmental laws we have. In today's risky atmosphere whistle blowers are a rare breed.

They will multiply by the thousands when they cannot be driven to unemployment and all of the unpleasant consequences their actions might invoke now. The result will be a far greater compliance with environmental laws and mandates by polluters and exploiters. This change alone will give the world a new lease on life.

A slower pace

The changes that will ensue from income security will include a slower pace, more education for the real joy of learning rather than out of the anxiety to get a better job, time to play, the opportunity to develop community relationships that will not be soured by our constant over-concern with money. These will be compatible with increasing education about and concern for preserving the environment.

If we travel, we will investigate and encourage by our demand the means of choice: bicycle, train, and the thousand-passenger cruise ship—not as a status symbol of the rich who can afford to take the time for an ocean voyage, but as an economical way to get there that binds us to our fellow-travellers on this earth, provides easy time changes and a pleasant environment during all of our days rather than more worship of the god of speed.

Summary

The most important effect of $30,000 per citizen per year for life, after the elimination of poverty and welfare, is the likelihood that it will stabilize population growth, even allowing the numbers to decline. We in the over-consumptive society will also reduce our demand by fair and painless means.

Other positive environmental effects include the saving of agriculture, reforestation, the re-establishment of cities as friendly places to live and work, and a huge boost to the cooperative movement.

Chapter 9.
All nations can eliminate poverty

We have selected the United States as our example on which to illustrate the effects of income redistribution on the economy and on the people. There are good reasons for this selection. All adults can vote in this democracy. We share many things in addition to the vote, such as culture, outlook, neighborly feelings, a shared and defended border, education, language, taxes, government, and a common currency, which the government controls. And we are all familiar with the Internal Revenue Service, which also returns subsidies and refunds to many of us.

A fair income can be instituted in other contexts, such as under a world government (when the world government we have becomes effective.) Or in a single state or district of any nation, or in any voluntary community dedicated to income sharing. It is never imposed by one political entity on another. This will be done by democratic means, not by conquest.

Other nations can do it

Any nation can install a fair income. The democratic requirement faces the fact that rulers are almost always the rich and privileged, who will not eagerly pursue this dream out of self interest. A history of equality and cooperation will make the Scandinavian

Table 1.
International comparison of income distribution, selected nations

Nation	GNP per capita in $US (1986)	% of household income in lowest 20% of population	% of household income in highest 10% of population	Factor* (Column 4 divided by Column 3)
Canada	$14,100	4.6	25.0	5.0
India	270	5.0	34.9	7.0
Japan	12,850	9.1	22.7	2.5
Mexico	1,850	3.5	36.3	11.0
Norway	15,480	5.0	23.7	5.0
Pakistan	350			(est.) 7.0
Philippines	570	3.5	40.9	12.0
Saudi Arabia	6,930			(est.) 15.0
South Africa	1,800			(est.) 15.0
Switzerland	17,840	6.0	27.0	4.5
UK	8,920	7.0	23.4	3.0
US	17,500	4.2	28.2	7.0

*The last three columns of ratios carry dates from 1971 to 1982. Source: World Resources, 1988-89, World Resource Institute, New York: Basic Books, 1988, Tables 14.1 and 14.4. Note that three of these countries do not provide income data by quintile from lowest to highest, and that comparisons are not of lowest with highest quintiles, but of the lowest quintile with the highest decile, which makes the factors in column 5 look artificially small.

countries likely prospects. A history of income security, not afflu-ence, will make former Communist nations likely prospects.

Even a dictator might find this program an appealing legacy for his people and his image. The United States may have to hurry in order not to be left in the dust of freedom and fairness among the nations. We can hope we will hurry for more important rea-sons.

India can eliminate poverty

Any nation that installs a fair income will eliminate poverty thereby. Even in India, the country written off by Paul Ehrlich in 1968, the distribution of wealth and income is little different than it is in the United States. Privilege has had a longer time to become entrenched there, so the differences are greater, but the percentages are similar.

This program would put unearned income at a livable scale in the hands of everyone in any country. No charity is needed. And income security would reduce the population problem in crowded countries at an astonishing rate. Table 1 shows the percentage in-come distributions in a few selected countries.

The rules for any country

Here are the rules that any country will have to adopt when installing a fair income:

1. Place all rent, interest, most profit, all gifts, inheritances, and windfall gains in a Fund to be distributed equally to all (children get special rates.)
2. Place all royalties from mines and other natural resources in the Fund.
3. Raise the prices of resources to an amount sufficient to insure an equitable distribution between present and future generations.

4. Place all royalties from invention except an amount deemed a reasonable wage in the Fund.
5. Place 60 percent or more of wages and salaries in the Fund because labor is a joint product.
6. Tax all income an amount which will pay for all government services and projects, thus balancing the national budget.
7. Treat a portion of proprietors' income as salary, and the remainder, profit, will be tax free for the first five years, subject to 50 percent tax for the next five years, and taxed 90 percent after year ten.
8. Place a cap on take-home pay that is approximately ten times the income of the lowest paid work in the society, with the excess going into the Fund.
9. Empower the national internal revenue service to administer the collection of these taxes and others and the sharing of income among the individuals and family units that are eligible to receive income from the Fund. This service will be subject to strict audit, legislative and individual oversight.

Resources that belong to all nations

After we have instituted $30,000 per year in the U.S., we will probably become a little more relaxed in our greed, and will sign the Law of the Sea treaty, which distributes among all nations the riches that lie on and under the seabed. It is also likely that we will look at the distribution of underground resources worldwide, and decide that the income from this great wealth, which is so unequally strewn in the earth's crust, should be subject to equal distribution among all of the earth's population.

As an incentive to participation in the fair income program, we would likely want to limit our offer, on a reciprocal basis, to those nations that had installed this program domestically. Such worldwide sharing from the resources of the earth would affect total incomes in the U.S. by a very small amount, but it would require a new rule:

10. When elements of the Fund are transferred to all people, nations concerned will have to install a fair income, and the revenue services of those nations will be subject to audit by international government. (The audit requirement can be met by the present United Nations.)

How can a state of the United States do it?

By popular initiative. The initiative would not impinge on the income tax collected and subsidies disbursed for federal purposes, including redistribution of income among the States. California, Oregon, or Washington, for example, all of which have initiatives, would not have to install their own currencies, or iron borders around the States.

Some rich people might move East, and poorer people move West, but the over-all migration effects would probably be smaller than those that followed the dust bowl and the Great Depression. Any state would become an example that could be duplicated elsewhere.

The Mexican border will be a problem

The Mexican border is already a problem. The problem is exacerbated by employers who want cheap labor. California can establish a residence requirement for participation in a fair income. If we lobby Mexico as hard for a fair income as we have for NAFTA, we can eliminate this problem.

What about communities and associations?

Intentional community members are free to abide by the rules of this program. Many of them already do. In an association

designed to transfer income, which might be any non-profit organization allowing unlimited membership, the rich who might be
involved would choose to live within the fair income guidelines,
and the poor, among whom Fund income would be divided,
would have to submit to some kind of income test, not unlike
welfare, in order to receive their equal share of the contributed
unearned income. Unsatisfactory at best, but this would be a start
toward universal application.

The nation is the preferred unit for institution of this program. It already has all of the apparatus it needs for implementation. All it needs is the law, which will be the subject of Chapter
Ten. We choose the state in the U.S.A. because Congress may not
cooperate until it has one or more examples. The federal initiative
will come through Congress.

Summary

Nations are the preferred vehicle for implementation of a fair
income. The U.S.A., for which this program was prepared, might
easily be pre-empted by another country that sees the light more
clearly. States can and will initiate the program. World government will culminate the process.

Chapter 10.
Politics: How we get the job done

The case for $30,000 per citizen per year in the U.S.A. is now complete. We have laid out its main characteristics, discussed its benefits, side effects, and flaws, and met some of the arguments against it. Most of you who read this book will be better off when it is enacted.

The problem that remains is political, and this is threefold.

First, we must educate our peers to the possibility and desirability of this action.

Second, we must enact the laws required to put it into place.

Third, we must make sure that government, politicians, and bureaucrats will not and can not put their hands into the Fund and divert its distribution to private purposes, government projects, wars, and other emergencies.

This last will require the vigilance that is the price of freedom.

The process

Politics is the process of enacting and changing the law. What we need in the United States in order to install this program is change in a number of laws. The tax laws will have to be changed, the Fund set up. The welfare and social security laws will need to be changed. Pension laws must be revised, rents and royalties adjusted, profits paid out 90 percent, inheritance taxed, and earned income capped. Many more adjusting laws will have to be passed in order to plug loopholes and insure the fair distribution of unearned income.

The technical aspects of law changing are well known, and can be implemented. The motivation and the mood, all the way from public opinion to the minds of our representatives in Congress, have to be operated upon first by a convinced minority, who by their activity and enthusiasm become a majority. Then we will find the candidates who have the courage to place significant change on the agenda, run for office on fair income as a platform, and when elected, pass the laws.

The odds against this are considerable

The political process may not be as easy to carry out as in "the old days," when public morality was higher, when millions of dollars were not required for campaigns, when dirty politics and character assassination were not widespread, when more than 50 percent of us went to the polls, when issues were more important than personality and charisma, and when, in fact, we took politics seriously.[1]

But not overwhelming

The saving grace of this scenario lies in three facts, all of which provide hope. The first is our evolving technology. Expensive, advertising-run television is not the only means for getting the message out. Millions of us are now involved in our own forms of electronic communication. We have our own computers, modems, e-mail, networks, and bulletin boards, and we use them.

It is no longer a prohibitive expense to produce a cassette, or

1. For a chilling description of the state of democracy in America, see William Greider, "Who Will Tell the People?" New York, Simon and Schuster, 1992.

even a videotape. These things can be passed around, and are copied at will. It is said that Khomeini took over Iran by sending quantities of cassettes to the people of his country from abroad.

Second, people are revolted by public officials who do not carry out their will. President Nixon was hounded out of office by Watergate. Spiro Agnew was forced out by unethical actions. Lyndon Johnson could not run again due to public revulsion over the Vietnam war. The Senate Ethics Committee rooted out the Keating scandal in the savings and loan debacle. Common Cause, a national political organization, has made it a major plank of reform to clean up campaign excesses.

We may be dupes of the media that manufactures our consent. But we also have a mind of our own on issues that affect us all. And we can get the word, and get the word out, by means that do not cost millions. Senate candidates Huffington (California) and North (Virginia) could not buy victory in 1994.

The power of nonviolent direct action

The third direction comes mainly from abroad, and is the power of the people in mass and public demonstrations. The reforms in the entire Eastern bloc of countries surrounding the former USSR, the decline of communism worldwide, the destruction of the Berlin Wall, the reunification of East and West Germany, and the breakup of the USSR itself give evidence that the power of the people in the street can overwhelm seemingly monolithic and safe structures of political and economic control. Our history is change, and the situation is far from hopeless.

The will of the people is powerful

We can change the law as we wish against all of the sophisticated apparatus designed to keep us subject to the will of the rich. When people are sufficiently aroused to put $30,000 into the law, they can also control the people who would derail the process by stealing from it for personal gain or by declaring a national emergency. In order to implement our fair income, a constitutional amendment may be necessary and is quite possible. The following scenario contains a few hints and guidelines. We are looking for natural allies.

People are fair minded

Before we get into the grit of self-interest, remember the sense of fairness of the American people. We have made the case that there is no fair way to distribute unearned income except to divide it equally among us. Few of us feel good about stealing from poor people income that rightfully belongs to them.

A percentage of us will become convinced by rational argument that income redistribution is the right thing to do. That percentage will be increased by a number of practicing religious people, perhaps not many of them rich, who will be persuaded on ethical grounds.

Self-interest on the side of fairness, for once

But there is a much more powerful motive than a simple appeal to fairness that will make promoters out of the convinced, and that, of course, is self-interest. We are looking for people whose self-interest will make it easy for them to work for, as well as opt for, a change.

Among these we can count *the poor*, who will be much better off under this program than they are now with welfare or a minimum wage. Then there are *the old* and *the young*, most of whom will stand to gain except for the few of these who are counted as rich.

Racial and ethnic minorities can be expected to join this movement out of self-interest. And *women*, who will become able to manage their homes, children, and work lives, without dependence on a male paycheck, will be active proponents. Now we are beginning to tap a majority of the population. But we have just begun.

We would all be better off

We have found that an unearned distribution grant to every family, in an approximate amount of $80,000 per year, would make them well off even if they did not work. Work could easily double that amount. Then we pointed out that people would be able to use this income to allow travel, sabbaticals, change of occupation, education, and many other items that would improve their quality of life.

We now have a very large majority. If even 80 percent of the population would find themselves better off under the new program than under the old, then 80 percent of the population might be expected to approve the change. It now begins to look as though our only obstacle is getting the word out.

Self-interest is deep and predictable

Commitment to self-interest is deep and predictable. Psychology suggests it, "human nature" demands it, we see it demonstrated on every hand as unions strike for more money and perks, as farmers lobby for more subsidy, as old people resist paying for catastrophic health insurance—in any of a thousand ways. We can count on self-interest to be there, and in this case to work for the good of the whole.

Of course self-interest on the part of the rich, a small minority, will dictate a campaign of advertising, disinformation, and vilification against the ideas and forecasts contained in this book. We will expect the hype.

Are we committed?

The depth of our commitment to $30,000 remains to be explored. It will be determined by the strength of the arguments we have marshalled, by their widespread dissemination, by the conviction of believers in fairness and self-interest, by the depth of our commitment to the environment, by the development of active organization designed to promote the ideas, and by the enlistment of activists to lead a campaign.

It is a question of being convinced and of having avenues of expression. It will require a demonstration of power from the people that is compelling to legislators. This may even mean marches, demonstrations, teach-ins, sit-ins, and every kind of non-violent action that has been shown to be effective.

Non-violence in every instance

The emphasis is on non-violent demonstration and confrontation because this is ethical action, and it is a proven, powerful technique that can be used to change minds and political positions. Activists will not have innocent blood upon their hands.

If you bash the police, you invite the army. But if you go to jail in any numbers, you strain the facilities, and the nerves of the tax-paying public. Besides, being put upon by the powers that be is one sure way of eliciting sympathy for the cause among the uncommitted public. Arrest will be unnecessary to bring this idea to the attention and active promotion of overwhelming numbers of the population. But overwhelming numbers will have to participate in order to change the votes of Congress.

Non-violent direct action is powerful

If it becomes clear that normal processes do not produce results, the techniques of nonviolent protest and action are available to those who would change social and economic systems. These have a long, proud, and often successful history—which is not taught in the history books. Gene Sharp describes 198 specific methods of this technique, each of which is illustrated with actual cases, in his book, *The Politics of Nonviolent Action.*[2] More famous advocates and practitioners of these powerful techniques are, of course, Tolstoy, Gandhi, and Martin Luther King, Jr. Income redistribution is an ideal issue for nonviolent action. And the United States is an ideal place to demonstrate its effectiveness. It is a reserve technique if petition fails.

Riots in the street are less effective

It can be argued convincingly that the 1965 Watts riots in Los Angeles, with their random destruction of stores and property, were at the root of the fear that promoted President Nixon's initiative for a guaranteed annual income. But war between the classes will be as unnecessary as it is counterproductive.

The Los Angeles riots of 1992 did not bring hope, but more repression. They were an outbreak of despair. If others in their later wisdom feel it is necessary to destroy property in order to make their point, we are very, very vulnerable to sustained, intermittent, and concentrated attacks of violence. This can lead to a fascist state. Few of us want that. I predict that legislators will be reachable by other means.

Human scale in the good life

Here and there we have references to the fact that giantism in politics and economics robs us of independence, power over our lives, beauty in surroundings, and grace in our relationships.[3]

---

2. Part I: "Power and Struggle." Part II: "The Methods of Nonviolent Action." Boston, Porter Sargent, 1973, 445 p. Sharp has a number of other books, which are equally illuminating, provocative, and relevant. Among them are *Social Power and Political Freedom,* Porter Sargent, 1980, 440 p., and *Making Europe Unconquerable: The Potential of Civilian-based Deterrence and Defence,* Cambridge, Ballinger, 1985, 250 p.

3. See, for example, Leopold Kohr, *The Breakdown of Nations;* E. F. Schumaker, *Small is Beautiful;* Kirkpatrick Sale, *Human Scale.*

Authors present tight, logical cases for the fact that we would be better off:

1. With small companies, which would be able to produce practically all of our goods and services;
2. With smaller cities, in which we would control crime and be acquainted with our neighbors, with whom we would decide our common fate in practically all aspects of our lives;
3. With small nations, none of which would be able to threaten the lives and welfare of others;
4. That we would waste less, consume less, and have a higher quality of life if we would, as our tribal ancestors before us and even down to New England town governments, control our size to manageable numbers.

Why we grow, and grow, and grow

I have little to disagree with in all of this, although I grew up in a small town in which there was plenty of backbiting, lack of social awareness, and a dearth of cultural opportunity. There are also disadvantages in being *too* small, of which these authors are probably aware.

However, none of them seems to sense the reasons for our propensity to size, or to give recipes for decreasing that propensity. The USSR has recently come apart at the seams (its constituent states are not small), and the Balkans are again at war (not to become small enclaves, but to enforce the rule of one or another minority on the others). Neither the dynamics of these upheavals nor the voices of sweet reason will prevail over our propensity to grow to enormous political and economic size. The European Economic Union and the GATT are going with that flow.

The reasons are aggrandizement

The reasons for enormous size are not efficiency, nor comfort, nor rationality. They are the urges to inordinate power, worldwide fame, and unlimited amounts of money. Greedy people can get only limited amounts of these inflations of their egos in small communities. We will not be able to control growth to unhealthy size until we are able to control these causative urges.

Redistributed income will control size

Huge amounts of money will buy power and fame, so a fair distribution of this single element, money income, will resolve this difficulty, and restore us to a human scale in economics and politics. We have here a project that will make sufficiency the norm, the accumulation of huge fortunes—and the power that goes with extreme wealth—impossible. We have here a system that will cure the failures of excessive size.

Summary

Income redistribution is an idea whose time has come. We have finally reached the stage where the excesses of capitalism can be seen by anyone who will take the trouble to look. Here we have approached income redistribution as a problem of fairness and justice, not charity. This has been a rare vision in the economic literature since the time of Henry George, whose sight was keen but too riveted on land to do us complete justice.

We have shown that income redistribution as a right will confer a net benefit on a very large proportion of the population. We may expect that the most dismal projections of others are unwarranted, that we will see income justice sooner rather than later, and that we will accomplish our ends by means far short of civil disturbance.

We will see a burst of activism among ourselves and our friends that will take us a long way toward public understanding of the issues involved. We are literate, we are intelligent, we have everything to gain and nothing to lose.

Keeping in mind the big picture of the U.S.A. as a whole, we can do a great deal in those states which have the initiative. Your best tool is this book. Give it to your friends.

We will set up a loose organization that will help with petitions, elections, constitutional amendments, and political campaigns. It will be organized by states, and may have a national newsletter in which we can consult each other, note progress toward the goal, and smoke out, listen to, and debate the opposition.

What is our time horizon? Unknown at this time, but the longest journey starts with a single step. The first step is to send your name and address to P.O. Box 2343, Santa Rosa, California 95405, and expect surprise.

If you want this project to proceed quickly, please write your personal recommendation of the book to your friends, and send it in along with the names and addresses of 10 to 100 of your friends. I will mail them out. You may help with postage if you wish. All profits from the book will go into promotion of these ideas.

We are on the road.

Appendices

Table 2.
Illustrative Taxes and Net Incomes for 1990 at a few gross income and investment levels consistent with the assumptions of this book

INDIVIDUALS (in $1,000's)

Gross Earned Income	40% of Gross EI	Investment Income	FUND Income	Total Income	Federal Income Tax 14%	State Income Tax 4%	Total Tax 18%	Adult Take-Home
0	0.0	0.0	30.0	30.0	4.2	1.2	5.4	24.6
1	0.4	0.0	30.0	30.4	4.3	1.2	5.5	24.9
2	0.8	0.0	30.0	30.8	4.3	1.2	5.5	25.3
5	2.0	0.0	30.0	32.0	4.5	1.3	5.8	26.2
10	4.0	0.0	30.0	34.0	4.8	1.4	6.2	27.8
20	8.0	0.5	29.5	38.0	5.3	1.5	6.8	31.2
30	12.0	2.0	28.0	42.0	5.9	1.7	7.6	34.4
40	16.0	5.0	25.0	46.0	6.4	1.8	8.2	37.8
50	20.0	10.0	20.0	50.0	7.0	2.0	9.0	41.0
80	32.0	25.0	5.0	62.0	8.7	2.5	11.2	50.8
100	40.0	30.0	0.0	70.0	9.8	2.8	12.6	57.4
150	40.0	30.0	0.0	70.0	9.8	2.8	12.6	57.4

Table 3.
SINGLE PARENT FAMILIES
(in $1,000's)

Adult Take Home	First Child Income	First Child After Tax	Second Child Income	Second Child After Tax	All Children After Tax	Family Take Home
24.6	15	12.3	7.5	6.15	18.45	45.05
24.9	15	12.3	7.5	6.15	18.45	43.35
27.8	15	12.3	7.5	6.15	18.45	46.25
49.6	15	12.3	7.5	6.15	18.45	67.05
57.4	15	12.3	7.5	6.15	18.45	75.85

COUPLES AND FAMILIES
(in $1,000's)

Adult Take Home	First Child Income	First Child After Tax	Second Child Income	Second Child After Tax	All Children After Tax	Family Take Home
49.2	15	12.3	7.5	6.15	18.45	67.65
49.8	15	12.3	7.5	6.15	18.45	68.25
55.6	15	12.3	7.5	6.15	18.45	74.05
101.6	15	12.3	7.5	6.15	18.45	120.05
114.8	15	12.3	7.5	6.15	18.45	133.25

Appendix B
A cooperative attitude

We have mentioned cooperation a number of times in this book as a desirable attitude in the economy, a movement from which we can derive pointers for the operation of industry and trade. Cooperation cannot be forced, as management tries to impose it. It is valuable in every aspect of our lives, and we may look forward to a flourishing cooperative economy when we install $30,000 per year per person.

Competition is the life of nothing

Competition is endlessly praised as the life of trade, the basis of our economy, the producer of efficiency, the driving force to excellence. It is pursued in all aspects of our life, from sibling rivalry in our families through all aspects of our education in the schools, including grades, prizes, honors, sports, and the choice of the best jobs.

We are individuals first and cooperators second if at all. Role models, politicians, teachers, parents, and peers impress on us the use and value of competition. We are forced to participate competitively in every aspect of our lives. Since there is only one winner in most situations, 99 percent of us are losers. We are a nation of losers. And the cost to our psyches is great.

Appendix B: A cooperative attitude

Who analyzes competition?

Occasionally there is a forthright psychologist who addresses the problems in our lives occasioned by competition. Most of the profession simply treat our symptoms. Such an analyst is Alfie Kohn, sometime lecturer at Tufts University, whose book, *No Contest; The Case Against Competition*,[1] details the ways we lose by maintaining this national attitude. It is an excellent book.

Cooperation is another way

Cooperation is another way of living and working in the world. It comes from a religious ideal: brotherhood. We usually think it cannot be applied to our everyday working lives, which are based on scarcity, power, and control, and are epitomized as "Me first, the Devil take the hindmost."

Cooperation requires a conversion from current attitudes. It is based on almost all religious teachings—loving thy neighbor, treating even the stranger as a brother, and sharing with others as if they were family.

We have not tried to convert you here to the cooperative attitude. We have, however, searched the cooperative experience for clues as to how we may run the economy in a cooperative manner. We may take intentional cooperative communities as models.

Income in the community

The distribution of income is one of the important aspects of living and working in a cooperative community. Every such community deals with this question. Guidelines for income distribution, both within communities and in the larger capitalistic system, are essential.

1. Boston, Houghton Mifflin, 1986, 257 pp. $7.95. Kohn and I are both members of intentional communities, 3,000 miles apart and unrelated.

Homes

Resident intentional communities (groups that come together in order to build a community) must have land.[2] Founders may put up the money to buy land on an equal basis or some other formula such as a gift from a member or an outsider. If it is donated by a member, this may be on the basis that every member of the community has to donate all assets to the group.

The donor may reserve privileges, from living in the largest house to retaining ownership of the whole. In the latter case, power is unequal and members can be removed by the owner. If the land is given without strings, the donor may develop second thoughts, which may manifest in rancor if things don't go as he or she had planned.

If the land is bought on an equal basis by a small group of founders, means have to be devised whereby future members of the group take over and share equally in the ownership, or they may decide to live with inequality.

All of these questions relating to assets and income are likely to be addressed by the community. If members do not discuss these questions and come to acceptable decisions, the community will probably founder.

Assets and incomes

Assets (things owned) are included in these discussions even though they are not income, until or unless they are converted from one ownership to another. They trail a cloud of income, which accrues to owners periodically in the form of rent, interest, dividends, and royalties. If these incomes are paid, they will be recognized as income. If they are simply accrued, or if they are not paid and should be imputed, they are likely to cause problems.

2. We will use "communities" in the remainder of this chapter to refer to such groups. We don't mean by the term, then, churches, neighborhoods, cities, political parties, or other chance and occasional meetings of people.

The income from assets may remain in the hands of former owners, in which case these former owners will continue to own the assets; or it may be divided among members of the community, or be given to good causes, or some combination of these.

The point is that members of intentional communities have to think about where the income from assets should go. They are better prepared than most of us to think about this question in the larger society.

Benefits beyond income

There are the intangible benefits of the situation. All sites within the land are not equal. One will have a beautiful view. Another will be close to the garden, or the pond, or child care, or the barnyard, or industrial noise. Compensation may be arranged in terms of larger space, or a lower entrance fee, or a higher portion of taxes to pay, or some equivalence in money or amenities. Or perhaps members will swap quarters.

It is possible for the community to live with these inequalities, which are small; or for each member to believe sincerely that he or she has the best site on the place. If these questions are not addressed honestly and aired occasionally, feelings will erupt in entirely unrelated situations, like "Who took that tool I always use in the garden?" Community members learn to develop a wide tolerance for each other's idiosyncrasies, or they are likely to leave. The fact that many intentional communities have succeeded over long time periods, and many communities are alive and well today, is evidence that they have solved these problems, which are mainly problems of income distribution among members. They discuss income openly and honestly, and they pay attention to the feelings of members, feelings which erupt around money.

These are exactly the attitudes and awarenesses that must be developed in the larger society if we are to make capitalism a sustainable system. They are exactly the attitudes and awarenesses that *will* develop in the larger society in our consideration of the $30,000 program.

Children

Residential communities are likely to have children. None that I know of pay parents for having children or pay children for just being alive. But many of them provide income for children in the form of services. They may provide school, a nursery, child care, transportation to school, places and equipment for play, wilderness, training in arts and crafts, a healthy attitude toward work, surrogate parenting, parties and gifts—any number of amenities that contribute income, stated or unstated, to the lives of the children.

Again, the question of income for children must be addressed in the larger society if capitalism is to succeed. The issue is closely linked with population policy in the larger society. Some of the same amenities will be provided in the larger society whether or not parents are included in communities, but cash income may have to be given if the parents are on their own. Welfare addresses this issue, but poorly.

The limits of community

The smallest size of community is mother or father and child, or two people sharing the same household. Next is the two-parent family. Beyond that, some of us in America still count our extended families as part of our primary communities. Then there are intentional communities, which may be defined as groups which have chosen each other, either for living or working together, and which take some responsibility for each other in terms of caring relationships and money.

Cities, counties, churches, unions, clubs, states, the nation, and the world in which we live take smaller amounts of our time and attention, make smaller drains on our resources than may our primary groups (but they may also cost us more, if we dedicate our lives to them). We avoid taxes and dues and charitable giving as we would the plague, and as we have the strength.

My neighbor?

Jesus was asked, "Who is my neighbor?" He responded with the story of the Good Samaritan, who picked up a stranger who had just been robbed and thrown in the ditch, set him on his horse, and took him to an inn. This is not a story that fits with the attitude of the modern capitalist, even one who indulges in charity or welfare. But in order to make capitalism fit with the image of a human being, we will have to expand our attitudes about the limits of our communities.

Work

In industrial plants that have been converted to ownership and control by their workers (there are many), and those that have been started to run as worker cooperatives, the question of a proper income distribution has to be answered. Managers are almost always paid more, but not by factors of 5,000 or 10,000 that adorn the organization of the modern American corporation. The factor is more likely to be five or ten, without the zeroes. These salaries of the highest paid are arrived at in communities through discussion and decision as to what is fair. And the managers who work for these salaries are highly competent as well as content with their compensation. Highly paid corporate executives will have to lower their income sights when cooperative values are adopted by the body politic.

Unearned income

Inheritance usually takes place by means of assets, not income, unless it is in the form of a trust. But when the beneficiary receives the assets, they are at that point income to that person.

This income is not earned, it is a gift. Communities treat gifts in their policies on the contribution of assets, which may allow none or a portion of the gift to remain with the member.

All or part of an inheritance received by a member of the community may be used for capital construction or replacement, investment, or spent as income. Given the mores of the society in which we live, we tend to invest assets and spend the income from them.

In the larger society, the U.S. government is extremely tender toward people who give and receive inheritances. Individuals can leave $600,000 estates without tax, couples can devise twice that much without paying the rest of us a nickel in tax. Community values will probably change this attitude of government generosity when they become dominant. The security provided by communities will become general, and estates will not be as clutched by individuals as they are now.

The jobless and homeless

Job security is usually provided by worker-owned businesses. Home security is usually provided by intentional communities. There are no jobless or homeless in community. Intentional communities may reduce their standards of living in order to provide these securities, but this is easier to do than watch your fellow community members suffer. Communities are like families in this regard, and family values apply to every member.

Work and income

In the larger community that is our nation, we will provide against joblessness and homelessness by a guaranteed annual income, given as a right to everyone regardless of work. Work will still be rewarded with earned income in addition to the guarantee. This is the only posture that is consistent with a human economy and a sustainable capitalism—and with community values. And, I might add, with any religion.

Appendix B: A cooperative attitude

Jobs and a cooperative economy

Jobs are the most important element of the economy to workers in unrestrained capitalism. The threat of unemployment pits labor against owners, free trade, the environment, and many requirements of sustainability. With a guaranteed annual income of sufficiency, this litany will subside in importance. Our attitudes toward work will change. Worker-owned plants will not be tempted to move to countries with cheap labor in order to enhance the bottom line. Other considerations, like home and community ties, the costs of moving, the local infrastructure, the destabilization of opportunity, will take precedence.

These costs of moving, together with returns that will be limited by community values, will deter non-worker capitalists who seek to profit by exploiting the people of low-wage countries while infecting them with the virus of consumerism.

With work forces that change slowly, worker owners have to be flexible toward the work they do. Technological change and competition may force them to change their product mix, their training, and their capital requirements drastically. Their ingenuity will match these challenges, but our attitudes toward occupation will have to change.

Group independence and resourcefulness will become powerful motives in our working lives. Anyone can learn to do anything. No one is only a type setter or a machine stamper or a secretary. We are all human beings, with infinite learning capacity.

Capital is available

The availability of capital is presently a limiting factor in either the development of worker-owned industry or community-based housing. Standard capitalist propaganda has it that risk capital has to be offered the prospect of high return or it won't come out in the sunshine. No one wants to invest in stock, bonds, or properties unless they think they will make a killing—well, at least a very good return.

So we have to think about this aspect of human greed. The answer to the availability of capital is to allow anyone to make money as fast as he or she can or wants to up to a limit. And the limit should be the amount of income everyone else is allowed to receive without earning it.

Assets of $500,000

This means that persons may each invest and keep the income from $500,000, if their average rate of return is 6 percent, and the average distribution from all unearned income is $30,000 per year. They can invest more, and "earn" more on their money than the limit, but in order for the limit to be a limit, they will be taxed any excess unearned income they receive beyond the limit. That excess will be returned to the rest of us as part of everyone's unearned income. This will probably vastly *increase* the amount of money available for investment, and will spread the basis of capitalism to everyone—a goal that is desirable in the eyes of most of us.

More important in the start-up of new enterprise and in the buy-out of previously privately owned shops will be the ability of workers to provide their own capital when the cooperative ethic takes over. We will find that individuals are easily able to save and invest $10,000 to $20,000 in their workplaces when the returns from unearned income in the general economy are shared equally.

Capital will be hired by the workers, not continue as an automatic shoveler of profit into the hands of the few. Cooperatives will thus provide their own equity, and upon this basis of risk containment, they will be able to borrow any additional capital they may need from the banks.

Cooperatives will be plentiful

Cooperatives are not now, but will become the People's Capitalism. Cooperative work and home ownership are presently starved for capital because the sources of capital are tied up in the hands of a small number of powerful people, who want to keep it that way.

There are exceptions, mostly in the world of non-profit organizations dedicated to the promotion of cooperatives, in those who pool their own resources to start or take over falling enterprises, and in the Cooperative Bank, which Congress has established, and, as one might expect, has starved for funds. The Grameen Bank of India, the South Shore Bank of Chicago, and the Caja Laboral of Spain are outstanding exceptions to the rule of capitalist banks.

This physical constraint on the development and spread of cooperatives places no limitation whatsoever on the dissemination of the cooperative attitude and ideal. We are as free to educate as we are to talk. And the sooner we do this job, the sooner we will arrive at a sustainable economic system.

Summary

Cooperative housing and enterprise require those who participate to consider the distribution of income. Standard capitalists want no one to touch this area of the system. But private capitalism is doomed, because it destroys the humanity of its operators and the environment on which it is based. State capitalism (socialism or communism) has also failed almost everywhere it has been planted.

Cooperative, or people's capitalism, is therefore likely to succeed private capitalism. It is probably, in fact, the only viable option we have left.

The ethics of cooperative capitalism include treating every person as equal and with dignity, sustainability unto the seventh generation and beyond, the collection and equal distribution of unearned income, and a population policy based on carrying capacity and accepted through income incentives.

Those who are already in the cooperative movement, and others who seek a humane and sustainable economy, would do well to educate us all as rapidly as possible. The goal is to make cooperative ethics the law of the land.

Bibliography

Alexander, Christopher, et al. *A Pattern Language*. New York: Oxford University Press, 1977.

Bird, Caroline. *The Crowding Syndrome*. New York: David McKay Co., 1972.

Bookchin, Murray. *Remaking Society*. Boston: South End Press, 1990.

Boulding, Kenneth E. *The Meaning of the 20th Century*. New York: Harper, 1965.

Boulding, Kenneth E., and Martin Pfaff. *Redistribution to the Rich and the Poor*. Belmont, Calif.: Wadsworth Publishing Co., 1972.

Brown, Lester R. *In the Human Interest*. New York: Norton, 1974.

Brown, Lester R., et al. *State of the World*. New York: Norton, annual.

Chasteen, Edgar R. *The Case for Compulsory Birth Control*. Englewood Cliffs: Prentice-Hall, 1971.

Communities Directory, A Guide to Cooperative Living. P.O. Box 814D, Langley, Washington 98260. Fellowship for Intentional Community.

Curle, Adam. *Tools for Transformation*. Stroud, U.K.: Hawthorn Press, 1990.

Daly, Herman E., and John B. Cobb, Jr. *For the Common Good*. Boston: Beacon Press, 1989.

Durning, Alan. *How Much is Enough?* New York: Norton, 1992.

Devall, Bill, and George Sessions. *Deep Ecology*. Layton, Utah: Gibbs M. Smith, Inc., 1985.

Dominguez, Joe, and Vicki Robin. *Your Money or Your Life*. New York: Viking, 1992.

THE $30,000 SOLUTION

Ehrlich, Paul R. *The Population Bomb*. New York: Ballantine Books, 1968.

Ehrlich, Paul R., and Anne. *The Population Explosion*. New York: Simon and Schuster, 1990.

Freire, Paulo. *Pedagogy of the Oppressed*. New York: Continuum, 1983.

Friedman, Milton, *Capitalism and Freedom*. Chicago: University of Chicago Press, 1962.

Geoghegan, Thomas. *Which Side Are You On? Trying to be for Labor When It's Flat on Its Back*. New York: Farrar, Straus, and Giroux, 1991.

George, Henry. *Progress and Poverty*. First published in 1890, republished and kept in print by the Robert Schalkenbach Foundation, New York, 1955.

Greider, William. *Who Will Tell the People?* New York: Simon and Schuster, 1992.

Heilbroner, Robert. *The Worldly Philosophers*. New York: Simon and Schuster, 1980.

Henderson, Hazel. *Creating Alternative Futures: The End of Economics*. New York: Putnam, 1978.

Henderson, Hazel. *The Politics of the Solar Age: Alternatives to Economics*. Indianapolis, Indiana, Knowledge Systems, 1988.

Jackall, Robert, and Harry M. Levin. *Worker Cooperatives in America*. Berkeley: Univeristy of California Press, 1984.

Jacobs, Jane. *Systems of Survival*. New York: Random House, 1992.

Johnson, Warren. *Muddling Toward Frugality*. Boulder, Colo.: Shambhala, 1979.

Kinsley, Michael. "The ultimate block grant," *The New Yorker*. May 29, 1995, pp. 36-40.

Kohn, Alfie. *No Contest, The Case Against Competition*. Boston: Houghton Mifflin, 1986.

Kohr, Leopold. *The Breakdown of Nations*. New York: Dutton, 1978.

Lorenz, Konrad. *Civilized Man's Eight Deadly Sins*. New York: Harcourt Brace, Jovanovich, 1973.

Marx, Karl. *Das Kapital*. Washington: Regnery, 1987. (1867 ff.)

Meadows, Donella, et al. *The Limits to Growth*. New York: Universe Books, 1972.

Bibliography

Meeker-Lowry, Susan. *Economics as if the Earth Really Mattered.* Philadelphia: New Society Publishers, 1988.

Morrison, Roy. *We Build the Road as We Travel; Mondragon, a Cooperative Social System.* Philadelphia: New Society Publishers, 1991.

Moynihan, Daniel P. *The Politics of a Guaranteed Income.* New York: Random House, 1973.

O'Reilly, Brian. "Your new global work force," *Fortune.* December 14, 1992, p. 52.

Phillips, Michael, et al. *The Seven Laws of Money.* New York: Random House, 1974.

Phillips, Michael, and Salli Rasberry. *Honest Business.* New York: Random House, 1981.

Pizzigati, Sam. *The Maximum Wage.* New York: Apex Press, 1992.

Riesmann, David, with Ruel Denny and Nathan Glazer. *The Lonely Crowd, A Study of the Changing American Character.* New Haven: Yale University Press, 1950.

Rifkin, Jeremy. *The End of Work.* New York: G.P. Putnam's Sons, 1994.

Robertson, James. *Future Wealth.* New York: The Bootstrap Press, 1990.

Roszak, Theodore. *Person/Planet.* New York: Doubleday, 1978.

___. *Where the Wasteland Ends.* Garden City, Doubleday, 1972.

Sale, Kirkpatrick. *Human Scale.* New York: Putnam, 1980.

Schumacher, E. F. *Good Work.* New York: Harper, 1979.

___. *Small is Beautiful. Economics as if People Mattered.* New York: Harper and Row, 1973.

Sharp, Gene. *The Politics of Nonviolent Action; Part I: Power and Struggle; Part II: The Methods of Nonviolent Action.* Boston: Porter Sargent, 1973.

Sharp, Gene. *Social Power and Political Freedom.* Boston: Porter Sargent, 1980.

Sharp, Gene. *Making Europe Unconquerable: The Potential of Civilian-based Deterrence and Defence.* Cambridge: Ballinger, 1985.

Sheahen, Allan. *Guaranteed Income: The Right to Economic Security.* Los Angeles: Gain Publications, 1983.

Slater, Philip. *Wealth Addiction.* New York: Dutton, 1983.

Smith, Adam. *Wealth of Nations.* Chicago: Encyclopedia Brittanica, 1952. (1776)

Smith, J. W. *The World's Wasted Wealth, 2.* Cambria, Calif.: Institute for Economic Democracy, 1994.

Theobald, Robert. *Committed Spending.* Westport, Conn.: 1978.

U.S. Bureau of the Census. *Measuring the Effects of Benefits and Taxes on Income and Poverty.* Series P-60, Nos. 162 & 174, Washington, D.C.: USGPO, 1988.

U.S. Commission on Population Growth and the American Future, *Population and the American Future.* Washington, D.C.: USGPO, 1972.

U.S. Internal Revenue Service. *Statistics of Income.* Washington, D.C.: USGPO, 1992.

U.S. *Statistical Abstracts.* Washington, D.C.: USGPO, 1992, 1993.

World Resource Institute. *World Resources, 1988-89.* New York: Basic Books, 1988.

Index

157

Index